DATE			
NOV 15 1981			
APR 3 0 1993			

Pen and ink sketches, Jennifer Dewey

SEA OTTER

Jane H. Bailey

El Moro Publications

P.O. Box 965   Morro Bay California   93442

©1979 by Jane H. Bailey

ISBN 0-9602484-1-2

L.C. No. 79-50281

Printed in the United States of America

Library of Congress Catloging in Publication Data

Bailey, Jane H.
  Sea Otter.

Morro Bay, Ca: El Moro Publications
176 pp.
7902   790115

Phototypesetting & Pre-press Production by Padre Productions, San Luis Obispo, CA

Dedication

To Don for his judgment, opinions, and patience without end.

And thanks to:

The reference librarians of the San Luis Obispo City-County Library, the biologists of the California Department of Fish and Game laboratory in Morro Bay, the Friends of the Sea Otter (Box FF, Carmel, California, 93921), and Glen Bickford of Morro Bay, always generous with his knowledge, memories, photographs.

CONTENTS

WHO are the otter's enemies? Friends?
IS THERE a solution to the controversy?
WHO are the otter's guardians today?
SINCE he went to sea has the otter found peace?
WHAT is in store for this unique mammal with arresting behavior, temperament? A mammal capable of designing a pair of tools, devoted to his own kind, and individualistic to the extreme?
WHEN his expanding colony reaches man's famous mecca for clams — the Pismo and Oceano beaches — what turn will the struggle take?

—Jane H. Bailey, author,
THE SEA OTTER'S STRUGGLE
(Follett, 1973)

FOREWORD

THE SEA OTTER'S STRUGGLE, as written in 1969, was intended mainly to inform young students about one of our coastal sea's most fascinating creatures. As it turned out, the book proved equally interesting to adults.

For that reason, in this revised edition I have updated and expanded sea otter research with a more comprehensive readership in mind.

The passing decade has seen exciting advances in information in the natural world that were heretofore undreamed of. Photography has improved via telescopic lenses, giving us television and movie viewers such intimate glimpses of animal behavior that humans have become veritable voyeurs, leaving little privacy to animals, birds, fishes.

We are no longer surprised to see the porpoise doing a human's bidding under Navy training crews. And the killer whale: not only accumulating a repertory of learned tricks, but surprising the trainers with its own inventions. We see on the screen a chimpanzee flashing over a hundred symbols in *human* sign language as he converses with a human animal friend. Moreover, we see this mammal actually reasoning. More than once it assembled independently a pair of signs to communicate a message of its own creation. Another conveyed 500 symbols via a computer.

In writing to adults the sea otter's story and its behavior can be delineated more fully to include the violence perpetrated by humans against his species and against man's own species. And the story of the federal government's trespassing on a National Wildlife Refuge, slaughtering hundreds of otters by means of one more experiment with the hydrogen bomb. And the otter's sexual behavior, reproduction.

An adult can comprehend the puzzling behavior of the otter and his astonishing adaptation to a new element. A youngster takes these for granted. Finally, there is the decade-old conflict between the otter's fans who work for his population's restoration and expansion along the Pacific coast, and the sea-harvesting community's desire to confine the mammal to a segment of the coast. What are the roots of this controversy, its present status of solution-searching, and the prognosis for a solution to satisfy all concerned, including the otter himself?

Why hasn't the problem been settled, almost a score of years after the abalone industry called the attention of the California Department of Fish and Game to the otter's competition in the abalone fisheries? Of the two opposing lobbies, pro otter and con otter, seeking to influence the Department's management of the intertidal resources, how could the exquisite maneuvers of one consistently overcome the other?

In a relative nutshell the otter's innocent (or accursed) entanglement is described in the early chapters. Next, his unique physique and astonishing temperament and individuality. The middle section describes the intensely dramatic history of the sea otter family spread from Japan to the Aleutians and south to mid-Baja California. Then, its role in affecting history's course, including the Great Hunt's tragic fallout on one branch of the family of man since the mid-1700s. The final section, the politics, will detail the specifics of arguments of both sides, pros and cons.

The account promises to be as dispassionate a presentation as one puzzled observer can offer to another who just may be a bit more puzzled over this apparently interminable conflict blowing over the coast, especially over California.

SECTION ONE
IN A NUTSHELL

ONE

Meet The Otter, Clown of the Sea

IMAGINE yourself on a tour bus skimming along the cliffs south of San Francisco on Highway One. As you approach Monterey, where the itinerary allows you a half hour among the keepsakes of Indian, Spanish and Mission California, your driver spies in the foaming Pacific below a pair of marine mammals. Lying on their back, *they are playing frisbee* with a hubcap!

Would you vote to trade the half-hour of history for the competition below, as one busload did? Here was something to write home about: a pair of those seagoing teddies, called sea otters. *Enhydra lutris*, the only known tool-using marine mammal. Thought extinct by 1900, now approaching two thousand off central California's craggy shores. Each pudgy one a bone of contention between conservationists and fisherpersons, sport and commercial.

The playful critter that Jacques Cousteau frolicked with in Monterey Bay. Once shy, but now sufficiently audacious to approach a scuba diver, pat him or her with dextrous forepaws, then attempt to remove the diver's faceplate. Five feet in length, the smallest of all marine mammals — whale, dolphin, porpoise, sea lion, or seal — and the one likely to share the top rung of the intellectual ladder with the apt and beguiling Pacific porpoise.

Sea otter. The one that eighteenth century and nineteenth century fur hunters from over the globe harassed until the animals' own infants fled in terror to open sea at the mere scent of man. The one that genuinely committed suicide to keep beyond the reach of the hunter. The chocolate brown creature that refused to wait for nature to evolve his physique to the watery element.

Instead, in the late 1800s he shook California's golden sand from his paws and outsized flippers, and took it upon himself to adapt to marine life. Jumped, is what some of them did: temporarily in the north, and in the south they telescoped some of the stages of development that they had a right to expect. These chose the hard way of acceleration, apparently, and the Pacific's waters were benign enough to make the transition possible.

An affectionate and demonstrative carnivore, the otter is born and the otter dies off the California shelf. He avoids the strands like the plague — or did,   until the mid-1970s.   He works, frolics, loves, gives birth to and trains his offspring among those russet kelp seaweed forests a half mile or a mile offshore, where the breakers take shape.

What accounts for the recent wave of publicity washing over the sea otter? It's both his outsized appetite and his increasing population that make him directly responsible for an increasingly bitter triangular tugowar among the California Department of Fish and Game, the conservationists, and the sea harvesters (sport and commercial). But Enhydra has been protected through fifteen years of conflict as though armored with a King's X: unhampered, unrestricted, undisturbed.   But only protected by statute.

To exist in his chosen environment, the chilly 60-degree Pacific off of central California, the otter developed an astonishingly high metabolic rate. This compels him to consume a staggering quantity of invertebrates to keep the chill at bay, despite the fact that his unique fur *keeps his skin dry.* And, unfortunately, among the foods he relishes are several that man also fancies: clam, crab, and the fifteen dollar the pound mollusk, abalone *(Haliotis).*

The reason this cousin to the weasel is gluttonous, is that he is out of place, out of his milieu. He has a terrestrial physique, but he must generate a vast amount of heat throughout the twenty-four hours of each day: 5000 calories worth! Merely to keep even he requires this throat-grasping quantity, because he is without the least of gifts that nature issues an aquatic mammal: blubber.

Enhydra does have a do-it-himself insulation scheme, though: by blowing and churning the water he can pack his dense, silky pelt's 800,000,000 fibers with air-pockets. The result is an insulation on the order of the spongy fiberglass wadding used for insulating a building. It also endows him with buoyancy to raise his prone body high in his waterbed, thus reducing the degree of body bulk immersed.

The otter is characteristically quick-moving, jumpy, and almost constantly on the go. Even when "standing" high in the sea or pool to observe a human visitor, his paws may constantly be clapping below his chin. Moreover, even at rest his nervous body continues shedding its valuable warmth into the sea. Compare the 5000 calories he burns with a logger's 4000. Daily, an 80-pound otter devours between sixteen and twenty pounds of meat. A 180-pound human being with a similar need would eat all of this or its equivalent: one loaf of Italian bread, a cup of peanuts, a fudge sundae (without whipped cream and nuts), a pair of bagels, one pound of sirloin, twelve ounces of beer, one pint of chili with beans, and a pint of plain yoghurt.

It is this steep intake that has pushed the otter on a direct collision course with California sport fishermen for whom three otter preferences, clam, crab, abalone, mean recreation, and with some California commercial shellfishermen, for whom two of these mean a livelihood.

Five miles (as the cormorant flies) below the southern boundary of the otter's official refuge running along the whole of Monterey county and portions of Santa Cruz and San Luis Obispo counties, the decline of the giant snail, abalone, is in part the otter's doing. And quite possibly his undoing.

By the early 1960s his refuge was losing its capacity to support him with clam, cucumber, scallop, crab, sea urchin, worm, snail, mussel, abalone, squid, required by the voracious appetites of a growing tribe. The 1948 colony of 300 was approaching 500. In 1978 it stood at 1800.

Some of the otter's brothers left to seek their fortune beyond the range, only to stumble onto and feast in what man claims as his fisheries. Although he is an opportunistic diner, Enhydra browses without regard for the California regulations controlling man's harvest of some of the same organisms.

Periodically the California legislators and Department of Fish and

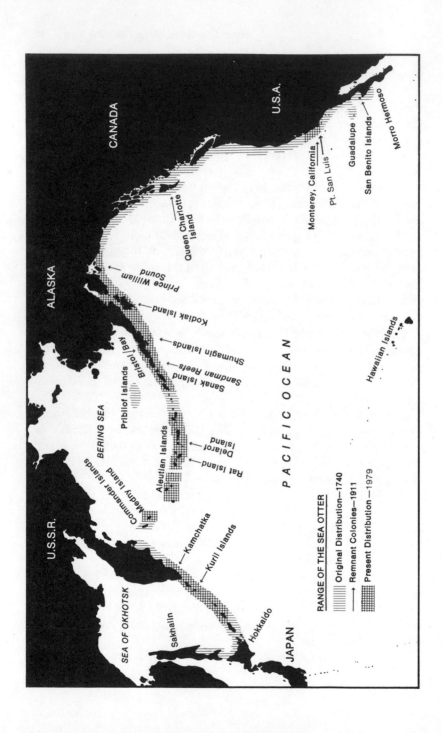

Game have tried in vain to produce a solution to the problem satisfactory to all sides of the triangle, as well as the mammal itself. From the early 1960s the sport pickers and the sport and commercial divers had been prodding the Department with the warning that the otter was invading a couple of favorite and most prolific red abalone fisheries lying in the southern half of the otter refuge and just beyond it. Proof lay in these abalone shells with a characteristic chink piercing their crown: the otter's trademark resulting from his dislodging the snail from its rocky niche. The otter flails the shell with a rock until fracturing it. Thus the abalone loosens its suction grip and loses the duel.

Meanwhile, the otter pursued his unique, devil-may-care lifestyle, roaming at will, blessed with federal and state protection. What's more, he was — and is — almost scot-free of natural enemies.

But he may have roamed straight to his Waterloo: in the path of about a hundred otters traveling south from their range lies one of the principal homes of the famed Pismo clam (*Tivela stultorum*). Annually the minus tides and gently sloping shelf of the Pismo Beach-Oceano Beach strips fetch thousands upon thousands of clam fanciers, their slim-tined pitchforks poised, their mouths awater for the succulent bivalve they pitch from the sandy shallows. The combination of the "clamtides", beach-buggy buffs, and a long weekend will find between 150,000 and 200,000 pleasure-seekers riding their hobbies over the five miles of sand and dune.

In 1974 the Department issued a report, "*Pismo Clams And The Sea Otter*,"[1] that blew the whistle on the little playboy. Here was proof of his foraging on the Pismo clam. The locales: Monterey Bay's Moss Landing and Estero Bay's Atascadero Beach (between the towns of Morro Bay and Cayucos, San Luis Obispo county. See map). Recorded clam densities in randomly chosen plots in the intertide of three other Monterey county localities, the documenting of clam reproduction and densities, *and* the presence of the otter, combined to produce damning evidence of the seagoing weasel's muscling in on the Pismo clam resource. It did not record the human invasion, but that was not the subject of this report.

Unfortunately for Enhydra, most of his forty diet selections leave evidence of the quantity he consumes. Like the boy fond of corn on the cob and drumsticks, he cannot hide the evidence of the number he disposed of. In the case of the clam, its otter-fractured shells lay exposed on the beaches both intertidally and subtidally, soon after the otter arrived in their vicinity. "Humans take away their evidence," as one man puts it, and yet the otter again makes a characteristic fracture that's a giveaway.

By the time this report was made public the ninety otters of the pioneering front wending south were believed within two or three years of Pismo Beach-Oceano Beach. This calculation by the Department is not a firm one; no one knows how to reckon the zigzag, to and fro, course Enhydra takes — not yet does anyone know. Another group, 140, followed closely on their flippers. The report corroborated the theory of many sea-harvesting folks in that vicinity, and drove the city fathers and many residents of the tourist town of Pismo Beach to their typewriters to ask the government to give the state authority to trap and remove the otters, keeping them north of Pismo Beach.

For many, this was not the first time they had warned their lawmakers of the danger. The alarm that the threat ignited cannot be underestimated.

California has more licensed sport fisherpersons and hunters than any other state: ten per cent of its twenty million population. A vigorous, weighty lobby to influence programming, management, regulations. For more years than the Department has endeavored to find a solution, the otter competition in the abalone beds has so infuriated some commercial abalone pickers that they have shot the mammals, despite the threat of a $1000 fine and jail sentence of one year. The scuba-diving sport harvesters were also suspect. During the 1960s and 1970s otter carcasses washed ashore carried wounds such as a diver's gun would produce, increasing in numbers as the late Seventies arrived.

TWO

The Conflict Rages

THE "OTTER SIDE," is convinced of the vital position Enhydra occupies in the web of intertidal and subtidal marine life, and it insists that he should be permitted to expand to the extent of his historic boundaries "in the best interest of our Pacific coastal water's ecological integrity". This would be midway down Baja California and north presumably to Canada, up its coast until melding with the northern otter.

The otter's supporters cite the opinions of biologists in agreement that the otter (northerner and southerner) benignly influences the nearshore marine community. By eating the invertebrate grazers (e.g. herbivores such as sea urchins, abalone, kelp crabs, mussels, turban snails) Enhydra helps maintain the equilibrium of the seaweed community.

They point out that this balance, disturbed by man's "selective predation" on the otter during the 150 years of the great hunt, produced the aberration of a veritable mine of certain shellfish over the first quarter of this century. Without this intensive fur rush nature would have maintained her customary seesaw method of balancing the floral and faunal members of this algal community. The burgeoning of abalone was an imbalance, another result of man's tinkering in nature's bailiwick. Man had removed the abalone's predator, the otter, to the point just short of extinction, thus providing the abalone bonanza awaiting the early coastal settlers — the Chinese, the Japanese, and by 1930, the Caucasian — all in their turn.

The human pressures on all resources, not alone the western states fish and shellfish populations, are common knowledge. Examples are legion. Such is the pressure on the abalone that the number of sport and commercial divers taking abalones by commercial boat charter increased 430% between 1965 and 1974. This, plus a legal 250 day increase in sport diving days per annum. The ab fleet, 75 vessels in the 1950s, rose to 300 by 1974, and by the 1960s, 400 commercial divers were competing with one another. The year 1963 saw 505, while 1928 had but eleven.

Skindivers picking abs from the Oregon border south to Santa Barbara leaped 540% between 1960 and 1972. Moreover, January of 1978 brought a development undreamed of: California regulations decreed a future reduction of the commercial abalone fleet by attrition and by limiting commercial licenses until the fleet is reduced to 100 active vessels. New ones will be accepted in the amount of 5% of the licensed numbers in operation.

California's and Mexico's abalone fishery declined 43% between 1968 and 1974. As for sportpicker competition, on one June day in 1977 two thousand divers converged on the accessible half of a thirty-five mile segment of shore in Mendocino county, northern California. This is not atypical. Along the coast of Sonoma county a minus tide falling on a weekend will draw from 6,000 to 12,000 pickers, according to the director of the Department, E. C. Fullerton, "In 1970 catch records for Southern California party boats for skindivers: 82% of 23,656 dives was (for) abalone, lobsters, and rock scallops".

By 1972 the long-fruitful red abalone beds just north of Estero Bay (some five miles below the southern border of the original range of the otter as set by the state) were not worth the time fishing. The industry claimed the wanderers had totaled the fishery. The Department admitted that other elements besides the otter were responsible. Now to be sure, ab champions admit that the otter cannot extirpate the giant snail. However, the otter, without the restrictions man is under (providing man proceeds legally), harvests all sizes except those wee enough to lodge in reefy crevices beyond even the agile otter's whiskers and dextrous fingers.

"THEM DAYS ARE GONE FOREVER." Japanese commercial aba-lone harvesters at Cayucos, near Estero Point, California, c. 1911. (Michael Villa Photo)

Tempers and pressures continue to rise over this loss, for the beds had supplied many of the takes of some fifty abalone boats, some employing a pair of deckhands. By 1970 only seven boats called the village and harbor of Morro Bay their port — about ten miles south of the rich red beds off Estero Point.

The remainder went to work out of Santa Barbara, 100 miles south. However, according to a University of California study, be-tween 1940 and 1960 the center of the fishery had gradually become dispersed between Morro Bay and Los Angeles, finally centering in Santa Barbara county. (Midway through World War II the region was opened to commercial picking.)

For a commercial fisherman or a sport skindiver to peer down from the bluffs near Pecho Point twenty miles south of the Estero fisheries (or from Sunset Beach of Monterey Bay) and watch an otter grasp an ab or a Pismo clam in its paws and munch the sweet, white, luxury meat is galling indeed. It is the same for the processors of Morro Bay, reduced from several days of abalone processing (pounding, packing) to one processing day per week as a result of harvesting but one day per week.

By 1969 the Department had witnessed and had heard witnesses enough to undertake its most comprehensive study to prove the otter's decimation of the shellfish of the intertide: clam, crab, abalone. The aim of the five years invested in the close examination was permission from California's legislature to prevent the otter from expansion both immediately and in the long haul.

By 1976 each errant front of seventy or eighty otters was moving at some four miles annually both toward Santa Cruz, northward along the Monterey Bay Pismo clam territory, and more importantly south toward yet-untouched-by-otter shellfish country. The graver of the two problems was the latter: ahead of it lay the clam beds of Pismo Beach-Oceano Beach, mecca for thousands and thousands of sport clammers over many generations. Thousands and thousands of licensed, expectant, Californians, plus commercial communities of that region relying upon trade from those tourists for major income.

According to the aerial census of Spring, 1970, the otter population numbered 1040, well enough beyond its former endangered species status to justify making some management modification. The overall abalone supply was reasonably healthy. Although there had been a slow decline in the takes, so it is with most resources on a planet marching unnecessarily toward overpopulation for many generations. The housewife watches this march as she pays $1.85 for rock-fish per pound, for which her mother paid 25¢ or less — and she cannot lay the blame solely to general inflation.

It is pleasant to report that the California Department of Fish and Game and the pro-otter faction agree on one point: the sea otter's great esthetic value. They appreciate the delight that the mammal offers to thousands of Californians as well as the out of staters and foreign visitors eager to spy on this unique creature. The only other American locales guaranteed for observing an otter pod, or colony, in the wild are Alaska and the Aleutian Island chain. A few northern otters have been introduced in recent years to British Columbia, Washington, and Oregon coasts, but to catch a glimpse of these is still chancy. Many of the bluffs and shores are inaccessible to motor travel, too.

OTTER DIET of three dozen items includes sea urchins with and without spines, abalone large and small. The five-segmented shell is Aristotle lantern. (Jane H. Bailey Photo)

However, with the increase in both north and south branches of the otter family during the 1960s and 1970s, as well as the improved habitats built by man, the chances of viewing him in captivity are increasing, to the great joy of many. The federal and state (Alaska, California) governments have granted guardianship of otters to more zoos and aquariums. Tacoma's Point Defiance aquarium, the Vancouver, British Columbia, Stanley Park aquarium, and Seattle's municipal aquarium at the Embarcadero, shelter a handful of northerners.

In 1972 California made San Diego's Sea World surrogate parents of ten southerners, perhaps confident that the otter book of behaviorial and physiological knowledge would grow thereby and help the Department to fathom the highstrung, individualistic little mammal for more successful future management.

Also, the hope must be harbored by the Department and by Sea World that on one happy day the otters will take to learning tricks of showmanship as the porpoises and the whales have done. However, with the otter's rugged, single-minded disposition, and his freedom from the herd instinct or impulse, it would come as no surprise if he offers his own extemporaneous bag of tricks to his audience.

THREE
Taking Sides

THE OTTERS'S influential friends, principally the Friends of the
Sea Otter organization, frown on placing the mammals in zoos. Few
of these can support spotless saltwater pools or afford a chowhound
costing more to feed than an elephant. Even with an ample budget,
the survival rate in captivity is desperately low. A year or two of survival in captivity has been a stroke of luck. Weeks or months are
more the rule. Only two otters have survived more than six years —
or anything approaching six years: Susie of Seattle, and Gus of
Tacoma. He died in 1978 at the approximate age of eighteen after
living contentedly and in polygamous state, fathering several short-
lived offspring.

The membership of the Friends organization, headquartered in
Big Sur and Carmel near the major and originally rediscovered pod,
has long since proved its strength and stamina by fending off the
first official plans to crop the population. In their primary venture
on the otter's behalf, the combination of youngsters and adults
quashed a bill in a legislative committee of the state Senate, hands
down. Forged in 1968 with the help and urging of the 'pro-abalone'
forces, the measure would have permitted the taking of otters ranging beyond their refuge, then 140 miles in length.

The term *take* was too vague, too suggestive of death to suit the
Friends, who were well-informed about the myriad difficulties and

fatalities among the northern otters as a result of many attempts to transplant them.

In 1977 the Friends did announce that they had come around to compromising and agreeing to reverse their stand on transplanting a "limited number" of the mammals. They were mindful, too, of the 1969 Department experiment to move a handful of the mammals forty-five miles north, only to find many of them returning "home." And mindful of the 17% that perished under the ordeal.

On the plus side, however, much progress in capture and translocation techniques had been made in the preceding decade.

As if the badgered Department had not enough grief in its thwarted attempt toward solution, Uncle Sam dealt it an unexpected blow in 1972 with the founding of the Marine Mammal Commission following the passage of the Marine Mammal Protection Act. The Department was preparing to move and to thin the otters when the blow struck: a moratorium on the removal of any otter off the shores of the United States. With this double event the State lost the guardianship of the otters in residence off its shores and gained another roadblock to delay the solution of the local conundrum. Alaska also lost its sovereignty over the otters along its own shores, including those of the Aleutian Peninsula.

Immediately the Department petitioned the Department of the Interior and its new Commission to grant a waiver of the moratorium. In addition it solicited permission to undertake a relocation plan with priority to be given to the translocation of otters from the southern front to the central range to the north.

Time was of the essence, for the specter of these errant creatures approaching Pismo-Oceano was as frightening to harvesters as it was real. At four miles per annum, more or less, the hungry mammal's ETA off those shores was something like two to three years. And the wheels of the government mills grind slowly.

Over the three-year period in which the Department petitioned the Marine Mammal Commission, adjusted and modified its project requests, the Friends were appealing to the same body for more than a return to endangered status for Enhydra. They requested:

1. The natural expansion to the otter's historic range.

2. The recognition of Enhydra as a vital evolutionary component of the nearshore environment.

OTTER NET is used by DFG biologist to capture, tag and obtain blood samples from otters, which are then released. The 1978-79 research project found these nets safer for the otters than tangle nets previously used. (DFG Photo)

3. The establishment of at least one reserve breeding colony beyond the neighborhood of the oil tanker ports stationed at each extreme of the otter's range (by then, 230 miles).

The successes of the Friends of the Sea Otter lie not in the sheer numbers of determined, well-informed animal fans whose motivation could be viewly solely as emotional. It lies in the dynamism and accuracy of the briefs accumulated by individuals supremely aware of transgressions that greedy or careless man has committed against his eco-system century upon century. Since "eco" means "house" in Greek, it appears that ecologists, lay or professional, mean to make not only repairs and amends, but henceforth improve the maintenance system of their house and home.

The general objectives of the Department match those of the Friends, but it has a harder row to hoe, charged with the duty to maintain and to manage California's resources compatible with the wishes of both commerce and the recreationbound millions. Expectations of assistance by government for our individual and collective good financial health is our national heritage. The reason for the restoration efforts in respect to the Alaskan otter, between 1945 and 1970, was to revive the fur economy lost to overkill before this century dawned. That is another story. What the United States Fish and Wildlife Service biologists learned from these years of experimentation is the baseline for California and Alaska to build their own research and should save untold manual hours, research, and otter lives.

Like the Department, the Friends have consultants among biologists and sea otter authorities. They give and receive grants for practical studies, they have a multi-media public education program. The sky is the limit for their work, it seems — they even have conducted an aerial census of the otter pods, usually one of the Department's practices.

Following the 1972 passage of the Marine Mammal Act, the Friends, convinced that the otter belonged under the endangered status it had recently fallen from, organized a letter drive to the Department of the Interior's Director of the USFWS. They, their friends and other otter proponents across the nation — including the Sierra Club — submitted 65,000 signatures to both the USFWS and the CDFG to demonstrate concurrence in the question. Five signatures were submitted against the proposal.

In 1977 the Marine Mammal Commission classified the otter under the "threatened" status, which satisfied the Friends and the otter's other friends. The Commission must have agreed that the otter pods were living precariously, in danger of their decimation by oil spills, tanker ruptures, and water polluted by city outfall waste. Since the late 1960s biopsied otter carcasses had been revealing the presence of toxic heavy metals, like copper, zinc, cadmium, mercury. Also, DDT, PCBs, DDE, and many other varieties of bacteria carried by sewage. Furthermore, the Commission knew that the deleterious results of oil or soiling of any kind endangers the otter's life. This is empirical.

The 1970s had brought more and larger oil tankers to ply the shipping lanes along the coast, one hundred miles or so offshore. Oil spills from Santa Barbara to Massachusetts to England to France carried ample and tragic warning. An otter does not need a coating of crude oil, like a bird, in order to perish. He needs only an oil patch on his pelt, the seawater penetrates to his hitherto dry skin — and pneumonia follows.

Clearly in these times Enhydra has no business in any sea — or does he? Could this help to explain the fascination moving so many of the human species to expend their energy, time, funds, to champion a disarming fellow-being with a sword of Damocles of sorts over his fuzzy, clownfaced noggin?

The Department, in pursuit of a sea otter management program to maintain and to protect a viable population of otters in central California and simultaneously protect the state's remaining shellfisheries, petitioned for permission for a two-year research and management program. First it requested a waiver of the moratorium on the hands-off regulation on the basis that Enhydra's numbers were sufficient to be no longer rare or endangered.

If Enhydra's current population increase of five per cent per annum were not controlled (the Department claimed), it would soon deplete human shellfisheries such as abalone, clam, sea urchin, crab, lobster, and oyster.

Here is the Department's final, revised, proposal, dated January of 1976:

1. Experimentally contain otters along a 230-mile stretch of coastline between Avila, San Luis Obispo County and Miramontes Point, Santa Cruz County.

2. Live-trap any otters straying south of Avila and translocate them to the northern end of the range near Santa Cruz until the range is filled (via tanks of water in air-conditioned vans).

3. Translocate a few females north to near Santa Cruz to initiate a breed population away from the dangers of a massive oil spill in the center of the range and to slow down young migrating or translocated males.

4. Set up baseline studies near the northern and southern end of the proposed range to assess long-term effects of sea otter foraging on coastal ecosystems.

5. Capture otters for research or public display.

6. Develop a new management scheme when otters fill to capacity the proposed experimental range (in 8 to 10 years). Options then would be to curtail them by "culling," birth control methods, translocation, or to let them roam free and unretricted.

And here is the position of the Friends of the Sea Otter vis a vis the Department's proposal:

The Friends of the Sea Otter consider the new State proposal to manage the small California sea otter population by experimental range restriction and translocation premature! Much needs to be learned about the otter's biology, population dynamics and influence on the marine ecosystem before such manipulations are attempted. With a 1975 head count of only 1321 otters and aerial counts stabilized around 1000 (plus or minus) animals for the last 8 years — and with serious man-induced hazards threatening the isolated California population, the Friends of the Sea Otter:

1. Oppose the waiving of the federal moratorium protecting otters and return of control to the State.

2. Consider the southern sea otter a subspecies threatened to the point of endangerment and in need of increased federal protection as provided by Endangered Species Act of 1973.

3. Oppose any range restriction of the California population but support the capture of 30 otters for translocation to the northern end of their range near Santa Cruz to establish a breeding colony away from the major oil spill zone.

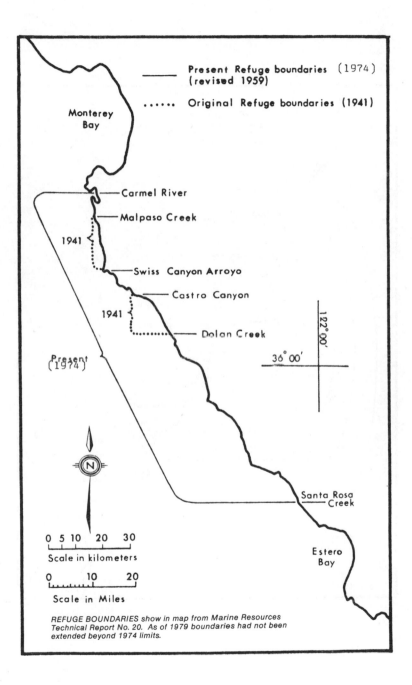

Present Refuge boundaries (1974)
(revised 1959)

...... Original Refuge boundaries (1941)

Monterey Bay

Carmel River

Malpaso Creek

1941

Swiss Canyon Arroyo

Castro Canyon

1941

Dolan Creek

122°00'

36°00'

Present (1974)

N

Santa Rosa Creek

Estero Bay

0 5 10 20 30
Scale in kilometers

0   10   20
Scale in Miles

REFUGE BOUNDARIES show in map from Marine Resources
Technical Report No. 20. As of 1979 boundaries had not been
extended beyond 1974 limits.

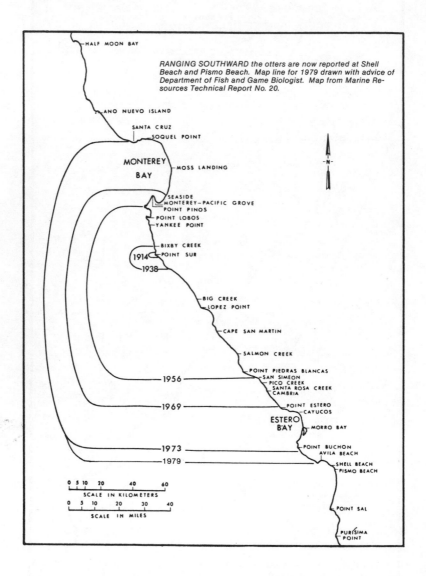

RANGING SOUTHWARD the otters are now reported at Shell Beach and Pismo Beach. Map line for 1979 drawn with advice of Department of Fish and Game Biologist. Map from Marine Resources Technical Report No. 20.

HALF MOON BAY

ANO NUEVO ISLAND

SANTA CRUZ
SOQUEL POINT

MONTEREY — MOSS LANDING
BAY

SEASIDE
MONTEREY — PACIFIC GROVE
POINT PINOS
POINT LOBOS
YANKEE POINT

BIXBY CREEK
1914 — POINT SUR
1938

BIG CREEK
LOPEZ POINT

CAPE SAN MARTIN

SALMON CREEK

POINT PIEDRAS BLANCAS
SAN SIMEON
PICO CREEK
SANTA ROSA CREEK
CAMBRIA

1956

1969
POINT ESTERO
CAYUCOS

ESTERO
BAY
MORRO BAY

1973
POINT BUCHON
AVILA BEACH

1979
SHELL BEACH
PISMO BEACH

N

SCALE IN KILOMETERS
0 5 10 20   40   60

SCALE IN MILES
0 5 10   20   30   40

POINT SAL

PURISIMA
POINT

4. Advocate establishment of a formal Otter Reserve, from Avila to Miramontes Point and including San Miguel Island with an additional warden force and appropriate protection plan to guard a basic breeding stock of the California otter.

5. Support further research on otters, to include tagging throughout their range; capture for scientific purposes, on a case by case basis, using Alaskan otters where possible; and the establishment and long-term monitoring of detailed marine ecosystem studies where otters are or may be, exerting an important influence.

6. Support the capture of a few otters for public display in appropriate institutions.

7. Insist on the use of hand-held devices for all captures except in an oil spill, where tangle nets might have to be used.

8. Recommend that necropsies of otters be kept broadly based and be handled at the nearest appropriate facility, by the closest approved investigators.[2]

And here is the long-awaited response from the federal government, granting both the Department and the USFWS permission for research and experimentation:

Effective August 1977, the Department was allowed to capture and to tag forty-six otters from four distinct sections of the range. No more than a dozen could be removed from the southern pioneering front. Captures were to be made only with the new hand-held nets, a recent California Department of Fish and Game refinement proved far safer for Enhydra than the tangle nets. (These would be held in reserve, in the event of emergencies such as oil spill in which time was of the essence and multiple otters must be snared simultaneously.)

By the end of the first year of the program some modifications were made by the Department of Fish and Game. The translocation project was postponed until the spring or summer of 1978, then moved to 1979. By late 1978 the direction was again changed with the decision to try a mock translocation and holding exercise. Presumably the exercise would simplify the true experiment when its time came. For the Department to detour in this manner demands another time-consuming go-around with the Federal Register, public hearing, etc. But the project is a first-time one, difficult to predict its speed with all the unknowns lying ahead of the researchers at the time the proposal was made to the Department of the Interior and the Marine Mammal Commission.

The Department's plan to seek "population dynamics" of the otter continues: documentation of secondary effects like effects of the otter on the marine ecology, and effects on the benthic, where the smaller invertebrates dwell and have their own effect on the algal community. This, in a limited section in the otter's southern range.

The United States Fish and Wildlife Service, itself granted a permit to tag thirty-five otters per year for two years and to rig some with radio-telemeter devices, for purposes of "facilitating recognition of individual animals", continues. The men and women working on this are headquartered at the historical Piedras Blancas lighthouse station in southern Monterey county, just to the north of San Simeon.

By the end of 1978 this agency was planning a meeting with California biologists on the vital subject of establishing a reserve breeding colony site. The California coast seems ruled out except for San Nicolas Island, one of the Channel Islands off southern California. The most promising locales, however, seem to be segments of coast along Oregon, of Washington's Olympic Peninsula coast, and British Columbia.

Now let us get on with the far more interesting subject of the curious, comical, winsome, touching hero or villain of this book: the otter, and where has he been all our life?

SECTION TWO
THE OTTER MAKEUP

FOUR
The Physique: Exterior

BEFORE discussing one source of our otter's jittery busybody behavior, i.e. his temperament or spirit, let's sort out his anatomy's components. This should help to understand his other vital and unusual features, such as his high metabolic rate, his thermoregulation process, and such phenomena as his stretchable hide.

We must remember that the otter is specialized at this point in his evolution to occupy the narrow zone of shallow water nearshore, even though he has become highly adapted to the marine element.

Catch sight of him on land and you will see a different creature than you see in the water. As expected of a land animal, he is furry and soft in appearance. On the surface of sea or pool, Enhydra is a melting chocolate or a well-licked gumdrop. Underwater he is a sleek corkscrew, whirling his way through the undersea forests of undulating seaweed.

It is this pelt, either sleek or fuzzy, which holds together the body so chockful of energy. If this body could expand to fill out its slipcover, it would have to stretch fifty percent of its bulk. The reason for a hide that gives (when newly dressed) up to 144%, must be for purposes of grooming — or developed over time as a result of grooming. And grooming is for purposes of survival, since the otter must have an immaculately clean pelt in order to keep warm, ward off the constant invasions of the cold water-cold air world he dwells in.

In order to keep groomed, Enhydra must be able to reach almost every patch of his coat. How can he squeeze and lick the water from the lumbar area above the tail if he cannot reach it? He can reach it: by tugging it forward between his legs. Actually the dorsal fur is so rich that it needs the least attention; a logical development. Mother Nature would arrange this, or else would have started Enhydra many generations earlier to work out a means of reaching that area for preening.

When the mammal navigates on land, poorly though he does it, his body contours alter to resemble, as someone put it, a sack of liquid. He becomes pear-shaped. He sags. His locomotion is to hump. A Russian biologist says that on land the otter moves with exertion and seems to be somewhat paralyzed. H. J. Snow[3], early otter hunter, said that the flippers seem to lack muscular power and the otter cannot place his hind feet flat upon the ground. When he attempts to walk, the toes are doubled back under the soles. Climbing onto a rock or a beach, he moves his feet alternately, but if in need of hurrying, draws both hindlimbs up under his body simultaneously moving by a series of quick jumps. This gets him over the ground at a good pace, said Snow, but usually damages the flippers in the process. He has seen the flippers bleeding from navigating over rocks, so believed that the otter does not travel any distance on land voluntarily.

Reminiscent of the kangaroo, the hindlegs bear the brunt of the labor of travel, with the front legs and paws seldom touching the earth.

However, the flippers are Enhydra's means of ambulating in the water.

His conformation suggests that he, too, was assembled by a committee: unmatched feet, a hide too large for his skeleton and musculature. The flesh held together by this casing is reputed to be both rank and distasteful and most edible, even tasty. The Ainu people of the Kurile Islands fancied it, as did Vitus Bering and his men marooned on the Commander Island when making the discovery of the otter in the eastern Pacific. Although they were starving, apparently the flesh was not only survival rations, but savory as well. And, literature indicates more communities liked it than rejected it.

Snow called it rank and disagreeable, preferring sea lion flesh. The Japanese and the Chinese rejected it, also.

The pelage is prime the year around — disadvantageous, for it helped to accelerate the near-extermination of this fur-bearer. (He seems to molt perpetually and almost imperceptibly.) It ranges in color from brown to almost black, with the ventral side a bit lighter. Albinos have been sighted and even photographed.

The pups are a yellowish brown, their fur fibers much coarser than adult or juvenile fibers. The important thing is that beauty is small matter: the pup's pelage keeps him afloat while mother dives to for-

NAPPING PUP is cuddled by mother otter in the Aleutian Islands. Pups remain with mother a year, apprenticing in survival tactics. (Karl W. Kenyon Photo, Bureau of Sport Fisheries and Wildlife)

age for them both through the markets of the sandy bottom. Pups look disheveled despite mother's constant grooming them with her claws and teeth (enough to fetch squeals of objection). If a pup's coat were to become saturated, doubtless the weight would swamp and drown him. Adults have drowned under these circumstances.

Gradually the pup's coat will modify until it becomes so dense a pelt that its fibers number 650,000 per square inch (or, as Ranger Interpreter Steven Johnson of the California Department of Parks and Recreation puts it: the equivalent of six cats) and 800,000,000 in toto. This is twice as fine as the precious fur seal's jacket. The Russians found the juvenile's coat takes on an intermediate stage at the age of five months.

Coarse, thinly-scattered guardhairs reach beyond the dense, silky underfur. They are dark or silvery-white. A white head and face worn by so many otters apparently does not denote advanced age.

Even casual observers notice the otter's lying high on the water's surface. With a pup on board, or the rock anvil on her chest, a mother floats high in the rocking surf, in part because of the buoyancy from the air trapped among the fur fibers. A larger than usual lung capacity plays a role in this, also. And both features offer the secret of Enhydra's successful permanent move from land to sea.

Head, legs, paws and flippers have shorter, less dense fur, which explains the otter's holding these as high and as often as possible above the water. A contortionist, he lies on his back, whirling his torso completely around on its longitudinal axis to cleanse his coat of foreign matter. As he does this, the head, forelegs, and tail remain in place above the surface! Thus, while washing off crumbs, he keeps his appendages as dry as is possible under the circumstances.

The average length of a northern male is 58½inches; his weight, 100 pounds. Snow said that a 4'6" adult yields fifteen square feet of pelt without limbs, tail, head. The female averages 55 inches, with a minimum of 72 pounds and maximum of 80. The southerner is smaller than the northerner: the female, 40, male, 55 pounds. During the tagging process in 1978 the California Department of Fish and Game biologists were impressed with the weight of a dead otter that they found: its weight was 87 pounds.

A pup weighs from three to five pounds at birth, and a yearling, twenty-two pounds.

FIVE
THE PHYSIQUE: EXTERIOR CONTINUED

TO BEGIN the otter's description at the top, with its head: it appears sleek and more weasel-like in contour when emerging from the water. When dry or somewhat dry it is in various stages of fluffiness. Two little pointed ears resembling a seal's more than that of his cousin the the river otter, lie deep in the fur and low on the head. These *conches* close automatically when the owner takes a dive, as do the nostril rims of the licorice-black, diamond shaped nose. The nose's exterior surface is granulated, like the pads of the fleshy toes of the forelegs.

Below the flat, broad nose lie two mustaches or vibrissae, one heading southeast, the other southwest. When foraging down among the rocks and sandy benthic, these are often in forward position, working position. In the wild they may be worn down to a stubble from feeling for invertebrates down below, but in captivity they may reach four inches in length from inactivity.

Sometimes the visibility is poor at the bottom where the otter-in-the-wild works. It can be (as one diver put it) as dark as a cow's stomach. Generally it is not, but observers have seen Enhydra in familiar, yet murky, water feeling about with forepaws and locating some of his favorite dishes without any difficulty. In shallows with silty floors an otter will dig vigorously for fat innkeeper worms of an inch and one-half to four inches. The silt rises cloudlike around his head,

BEWHISKERED otter moors himself by draping kelp stipes around his torso. Whiskers show little abrasion. (R.L. Branson Photo)

surely obscuring his vision, but for this dinner he relies successfully on his sense of touch. He browses during the night (mothers more than others), seeming to locate prey as quickly as in the daytime.

A pair of round black eyes also lies low on the otter's head, and wide apart. A female anthropologist claims that the only mammals capable of weeping salt tears are marine mammals. (This is to support her theory that *homo sapiens*, who weeps salty tears, was a marine mammal eons ago.

Enhydra's forepaws are the most dextrous of implements, with their sensitive little stubby toes, well-padded with black, granulated soles. Fur fills the crevices between these and the curved retractile claws. The paws can crush such shellfish as the sea urchin, despite the rather hard armor, or test, and its surrounding spines. They can grasp a mussel and pull it from its rock by tearing the extremely tough byssus, or threads, which moor the mussel to its rock.

Apparently the otter depends a great deal upon his sense of touch. He will circle a kelp holdfast (root attached to rocky substrate), patting it until coming upon a tidbit such as a turban snail. He stows this away and examines some crevices or hollows in the reef, searching pat-pat, until making a strike on a seastar, an abalone, a chiton, or must return to the surface for air.

Should he have too much to carry he can use the pouches, those loose folds of hide lying under the armpits, for shopping bags. Right-handed or left-handed? Seems to be right, but gathers food with both, stowing it away in opposite pouches.

The late L. D. Howard, M.D., of California, studied the forepaw's anatomical structure in close detail, perhaps because he was a hand surgeon. He was impressed deeply with the adeptness with which the otter caresses and grooms creatively and extensively. And how he picks up and carries an object. He found that the thumb is not opposable, and that the other puffy digits cannot be curled to any degree. Also, that the large pads of the palm fill the paw's entire palm region.

Dr. Howard saw that the tips of the fingers cannot be bent inward as far as to touch the palm. Even so, the otter can grip a large object between paw and forearm with good wrist movement and hingelike action. According to the physician, the forelegs appear similar to those of other mammals who use them primarily for fifty percent of their body's support.

The system the otter has of releasing an abalone's suction grip on a rock at the depth of fifty or one hundred feet, is among his most remarkable of skills. Many years ago someone calculated an abalone's maximum suction as some 300 pounds per square inch, forcing its predators either to lever its hold free or to surprise the abalone when its grip was relaxed, as when it is feeding. Man uses a lever. The otter dislodges the snail by pounding its crown with a rock until the blows shatter the crown area and release the suction of the foot. That the little arms of the otter can flail with repeated blows against the abalone through the water's resistance is one of the most astonishing of his accomplishments. Any human who has moved his body through water, even shallow water, can appreciate the strength necessary to move a limb rapidly against such solid resistance.

The otter has another, easier means of harvesting abalone, but perhaps it supplies him considerably fewer of the snails than his fracture technique. At times he can approach an abalone that is relaxed, shell raised as it browses on kelp detritus or on a stipe of the seaweed. Then, a quick swipe of the otter's forepaws can win an abalone without any work invested at all.

When the male otter lies on the surface, the penial bulge is prominent. The female in this position reveals the mammae at the base of her abdomen. A mother picks up her offspring with her clever forepaws, turns it about, and lays it on her abdomen within reach of her breasts. Or, an older juvenile approaches its mother broadside, reaches up to suckle as it lies at right angles to her in the sea.

Both the male and the female bulges are concealed by fur, but perhaps the otter must develop many eons more before these are deeply set, streamlined, like the mammae and the genitalia of the whale. Cetaceans left land for sea far, far earlier, and are more physically advanced in their adaptation to the sea. They have had between fifty and one hundred million years of modification toward their present environment, but the otters little time in comparison.

Moving down the anatomy we reach the hindlegs with their webbed feet, which often appear like sails awaiting a breeze: erect, flinching a bit now and then as though startling flies. Often when Enhydra lies on his waterbed, perhaps with paws shading eyes from the sun, the flippers give a rakish, clownish picture with one foot erect, the other prone. Probably the position is for the purpose of helping to adjust his body heat. Like a rabbit's ears, the hindlegs are not entirely fur-covered, and absorb heat from sun and air to accelerate bodywarmth when the body is cold.

It is this pair of appendages that gets the credit for the speed of some five miles per hour that Enhydra reaches in the sprint, belly down. One method of swimming is mere undulating, with flippers held horizontally like a whale's flukes and with vertical sweep. The Russians saw the otter as swimming — and fast — by bending the body only, and without moving the flippers.

At times Enhydra's method of speed swimming is a spinning, torpedolike style. It appears so effortless, like a greased eel, as Dr.

Karl Kenyon[4] describes him. Thanks to the films of Enhydra, many have seen his graceful navigation when he sprints belly down. He is considered a slow swimmer, his five mph compared with the northern fur seal, or the bottle-nosed porpoise, clocked at nine mph.

But, at any speed, Enhydra has the ability to change course with unbelievable swiftness — just one more of his accomplishments for survival in an alien world.

Physician Howard also examined the otter's hindleg, finding it specialized for swimming and without resemblance to the forepaw anatomically or functionally. A seal's fifth toe is as large and as long as its great toe, but in the otter's case the great toe is the smallest. The fifth toe on the outer side of the foot has become the largest and the longest, and it is for maximum sculling surface and greatest arc of motion.

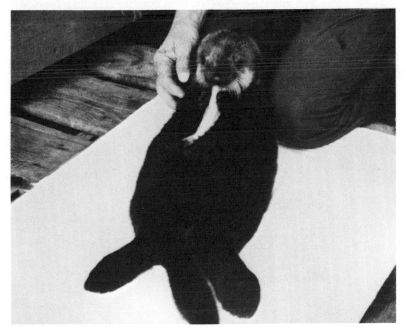

ORPHAN "HONEY" sheltered at Morro Bay, California. (B. Tyler Photo)

When the toes are spread in water for propulsion, the skin webbing gives the foot twice the surface area of the resting foot. The webbing added to the length of the two allows mobility for each toe. This would be impossible for short toes with limited webbing. The doctor explains that the feet are able to flex as far as to allow the tips of the toes to touch the sole. Also, allowing them to grasp an object. But, apparently they are limited to propulsion purposes only, thus far.

It does appear that the sea otter offers more than one aspect to the human: at times he is sleek, eel-like, slender, and again, fluffy and thick of head, neck, torso. Even his feet, that is flippers, present one picture one time and another picture the next time he is in view. Slim-flippered once, and of broad, webfoot appearance another time.

Strange animal, strange physique, perforce, thus far in his evolution and adaptation. The doctor sees a paradox in the otter's paws: they are more suitable for walking on land than for handling food, and yet the northern cousin seldom walks; the southerner not at all — at least very seldom in our time.

And now, the end: the tail. Considerably flattened, compared to that of the river otter, it resembles a stepped-on wide garden hose. It tapers quite abruptly from a uniform width of some two inches to a blunt point, and is less than one-third of the body length. When the otter moves leisurely about on the surface, the tail apparently acts as a sculling oar. Snow[3] believes it serves as rudder, having observed a tailless otter's erratic navigation.

SIX

THE PHYSIQUE: INTERIOR

SEA OTTERS are born with almost a dozen erupted teeth and others barely erupted. Eventually the teeth of many otters become lilac in color from a long history of purple urchin consumption, those *Echinoderms* ranging in size from a tennis ball to an indoor baseball. A diet high in these also eventually tints the otter's bones.

Enhydra's adaptation to aquatic life is hard on his teeth. Although some of those in the Aleutians browse on fish in the amount of fifty percent of their diet, most northerners and all southerners dine on a variety of some thirty-five species of invertebrates, many of them heavy-shelled.

Mussels (*Mytilus*), sea urchins (*Strongylocentrotus*), rock oysters (*Pododesmus*), are only a few whose shells work havoc with the otter's dentition. By the time many otters reach old age they have worn out their eating tools, sealing their own doom. Fortunately, the mammal is equipped with flattened, rounded molars. These are for tearing flesh; not for cutting or shearing. Even the canine teeth are rounded, blunt, and without the usual sharp point expected for tearing. The result of this type of dentition is that the otter tears and swallows with a speed consistent with his hyperactivity.

The otter's bite is vicious. An abalone diver who has entertained an otter on his boat's deck exaggerates, of course, when he says that the otter can bite your leg off. At least it is true that he can nip through several layers of foul-weather gear, plus heavy boots. It is also true that Enhydra gets help from his rock anvil in fracturing heavy-shelled invertebrates, but also grasps an organism in each paw and knocks them together to crack them open. Naturally he swallows shell fragments, passing them in the feces, but the Russian biologists believe that his system needs urchins, including the shell, for good health.

The Russians attributed diarrhea, weight loss, and other symptoms to the lack of urchins, because these symptons disappeared with the urchin returned to the diet. When Kalana gave birth to a pup in Tacoma's Pt. Defiance aquarium in 1974, she was prescribed an increase in urchin rations in the event that it was of critical importance for a nursing mother.

San Diego's Sea World's biologists believe that Enhydra needs hard-shelled items in the diet for the roughage because of his propensity toward enteritis.

Moving down we arrive at the voicebox for the otter's repertory of assorted sounds. The baby's cry is sharp, shrill, like a seagull's, and has been described as a human baby's cry. An adult's distress scream protests the kidnaping or the killing of a pup, and can be heard up to a half-mile distance. During the Great Hunt one man wrote home about the moonlit night that he rowed some ten miles in his skiff to the mother ship, an otter pup as passenger. All the way to the ship the hunter heard the banshee screaming of the mother pursuing the kidnaper. But he did not realize what the sound was until just short of his destination. Then, to stop the barrage against his senses, he tossed the pup overboard to its mother.

Another report described the sailors or hunters throwing overboard from their ship a pup whose incessant wailing made their flesh crawl. Another told of the noise rising from the nurseries (female and juvenile rafts). Although the men could not see the otters, they could hear the communication. When a mother surfaced after a dive she would give a shrill scream, and her pup would reply with a scream of its own.

A whine or a whistle (some call it a penny-whistle tone) can indicate frustration on the part of the young when mother is late with dinner. Also, pups whistle shrilly when in need of cooling down. Cooing is for courtship between adults, and Dr. Kenyon[4] observed a female chuckling in one of the rest-and-grooming periods during her courtship. Cooing also soothes the young while mothers groom them with teeth and claws, and cooing and grunting may result from a good meal in captivity.

Hissing seems either a warning or an expression of fright. Growling describes the warning sounds of a newly-captured otter.

Inside the otter is an extra long ribcage consisting of fourteen ribs, happily offering high mobility in an environment such as his. Doubtless it was developed to withstand a lifetime of ceaseless wave-buffeting since cousin river otter has no need for an extensive cage such as Enhydra's.

The otter's voluminous lungs and roomy thoracic cavity are consistent with his lung capacity in relation to body size: two and one-half times that of most mammals. The lungs, plus the fur packed with trapped air, support the animal high on the surface, reasons for which are obvious. Too, he can remain underwater for four minutes-plus. This would be necessary only in a situation demanding an escape dive, but most dives are for foraging, and one minute is the usual. When the otter intends submerging for an unusually long period and must retain more air in the lungs, he may tote a rock below for ballast. As to the escape dives, pups have been lost under the emergency of mothers' taking them down with them.

Enhydra has been recorded at depths of 144 feet, but 40 is the most common depth for foraging.

Liver and kidneys are relatively large, too. Development of the former is due to the great appetite and high metabolic rate, and the kidneys, perhaps because of the salinity of his shellfish diet. Also, his drinking seawater. The northerner drinks creekwater in addition to seawater. All of them press the excess moisture from their fur as they lie on the surface grooming, and presumably they drink this.

Predictably the otter's g.i. tract is exceptionally long and predictably his digesting process is brief. For those otters consuming benthic (not pelagic) organisms, travel through the system takes a mere three hours. His famous and infamous appetite requires between 25% and 35% of his body weight daily. This is one figure that can vary according to the report, and that's the truth. Nonetheless, all sides agree that Enhydra's appetite is immense, to say the very least.

ALEUTIAN OTTER resting on kelp-clad rocks, white face does not always signify an oldtimer. (Karl W. Kenyon Photo, Bureau of Sport Fisheries and Wildlife)

Adipose tissue — none as subcutaneous layer for storage as blubber. But juveniles and mothers are entitled to store a modicum of fatty tissue. The body temperature of the northerner: an adult female, 99 degrees F., and juvenile male, 100 degrees F. California's otter information is less complete, but on the way.

The heart is smaller than the river otter's heart, relative to his size. Probably this is because saltwater gives more support than fresh water does, so the need is not great enough to warrant a larger pump.

Life expectancy. A phenomenon obviously difficult to determine. Although captives are far from ideal yardsticks, the northerner Susie lived in captivity in Seattle's Woodland Park zoo for an unprecedented six years. In 1969 Dr. Kenyon estimated that a wild sea otter might live from fifteen to twenty years in an ideal habitat. This was after finding that the tooth and bone structure of Susie appeared to be those of a young adult at her death at about seven years of age. She had lived in captivity in fresh water since about a year of age.

Gus spent thirteen years in captivity at Pt. Defiance zoo, Tacoma, arriving as a young adult of perhaps four or five years old.

SEVEN

The Senses, The Intellect

WHEN a Yankee hunter of the 1800s wrote home from Alaska, "them otters have a human sense", did he mean perceptive senses, sensibility, or common sense? If he meant that Enhydra's combined senses cooperate to move his intellect, then that unlettered pioneer was on the right track.

The senses provide the stimulation of an experience by communicating with the brain. The brain either registers the message, or responds with some form of action. Considered singly, here are the senses giving the otter both his superficial sensations and his capacity to respond mechanically, emotionally, intellectually.

VISION: it is not acute. Someone said that the otter does not believe his own eyes. Yet he forages successfully for benthic invertebrates in a daytime murkiness, as well as during the night. Probably knows his territory, but there is one other feature which helps him with this — whiskers.

Observers say that the mother otter will scull about with her babe on her abdomen, her head turned so that one eye is beneath the surface casing the marketplace. Finding something to her liking, she will duck from beneath the pup, leaving him afloat as she does her shopping for them both.

HEARING: not very sharp either.

SMELL: efficient, and apparently serves him accurately enough. In the north, when men hunted Enhydra on land, they were sure to approach him upwind. At the first sight of Bering and his Russian crew, the otters were not frightened. Bering described them as genial, saying that his marooned men could approach the animals as close as five or ten fathoms (thirty or sixty feet).

But that tameness would soon change.

Early in the Great Hunt otters were attracted to campfires. But soon the mere catch of the scent of a fire four or five miles distant would send them fleeing in another direction. Even litter left behind by the hunters threw the otters into a panic. They would leave the shore on catching the smell of a human footprint in sand or shingle and, until the tide had washed in and out many times, the otters avoided those beaches.

TASTE (in the sense of preferences in food, drink): the otter is an opportunist, like a human, eating his favorites when available, and less-relished items when they are not. In abalone country a single abalone saves Enhydra a great many dives for organisms of smaller biomass: clams, mussels, spiny urchins, turban snails, crabs, cucumbers, chitons, fat-innkeeper worms, tubeworms, and most of some thirty items.

The biomass of an abalone of eight and one-quarter inches and weighing two pounds, three-tenths, equals sixty-three small mussels, thirty-one small purple urchins, two large gaper clams, or three red urchins. Consider how much pawing through bottom silt fetches the equivalent in innkeepers. Or snails, by exploring the kelp.

Four southern otters surviving the move to San Diego's Sea World exhibited a preference for frozen eastern clams and crabs over abalone trimmings and squid. The southerner does not prey on fish, like some of the northerners, but he fancies the squid (*Loligo opalescens*) which spawns in Monterey Bay. Amchitka Island otters choose the sluggish fishes, globefish and Irish lord, for half their rations. That Enhydra needs variety there seems little doubt: according to the Russians their four captives showed their rejecting a monotonous diet to the point of fasting! Of course, this resulted in the risky lowering of the body heat and a reduction in activity.

The Russians' experiment during the 1930s found individual taste diverse to the extreme: only one captive accepted a bit of bread and biscuit, and then only after ignoring these for some time. Another bolted down bits of fur seal. They ate beef readily, and only a few ate salted fish, but reluctantly. They more willingly accepted soaked salted fish, with some of the freshwater-pool captives eating it with particular eagerness.

One otter avidly consumed a pelagic bird, fulmar, preferring it to fish; yet he would not touch it before it was dressed. When the otters came upon a freshly-killed murre, they all started back in fright. Even when the bird was dressed and chopped they rejected it. Customarily live birds frightened the captives. A small snipe flying into their cage stampeded them.

Even their manner of eating varied from individual to individual. Perhaps this individuality is characteristic of Enhydra. Among the members of a colony apparently one individual may be appreciably distinct from another. One would expect uniformity in the rearing of the southern otters and the same for the northern branch. But one southerner may be dining on clams in one spot and at a short distance away another otter may be dining on urchins. One of the Department of Fish and Game biologists says that these two may never have eaten or had experience with the shellfish that the other is foraging on.

All of the southern range is home to the abalone. Yet, when some filmmakers set up a situation to lure some otters to demonstrate how an otter shatters an abalone to release its grip on the rock, the otter that appeared onstage was ignorant of the procedure expected of him!

The abalone was present, the rock was present, and the hungry predator was present. But the situation fizzled.

TOUCH: it seems easier to divide the otter's tactile sensory skills into two types, the mechanical and the complex intellectual responses. Acts of grooming (e.g. pressing a fold of the pelage between paws to wring out moisture) or such an accomplishment as pounding shellfish with a rock either below or on the surface, can be interpreted as mechanical capacity. So can the nocturnal (or diurnal) foraging in the depths with his facile paws and dependable vibrissae, whiskers. By patting rocks, depressions in cracks, and the kelp canopies, the otter shows his sense of touch may serve him better than his vision under certain circumstances.

One southern otter approached a photographer on the surface to fiddle with his faceplate. A young woman, scuba diving with her husband in a Monterey Bay locale, felt hands patting her legs, and reasoned that her mate was growing amorous at the bottom of the sea. The hands proved to be an otter's forepaws as he explored his latest discovery: a modern mermatron.

The otter's dexterity makes it difficult for humans to resist translating some of his activities into the anthropomorphic. In mating play, both the male and the female use their forepaws for caressing. Dr. Kenyon[4] disturbed a pair resting on a rock, and the female warned the male of his approach by pressing her paws against his face, neck, and chest. This failed to rouse him, so she crawled on top of him. It was not until she pressed her body against his back that she moved the male to follow her into the haven of the sea.

Outside of mating play, a pair of otters might romp together in the water, hugging with their forepaws as they repeatedly plunge, leap, submerge, and emerge.

A half-dozen animals possess the coordination to use a tool, but aside from the primates, perhaps none manipulates a tool as the otter does. The female otter clutches the pup with her forepaws, lifts it into the air above her head (observers report this an act of joy). She will turn it end for end to place its muzzle against her breasts. And she has the capacity to drape a stipe of kelp over herself or the babe to stabilize their position on the moving water.

Adults living in the kelp forest neighborhoods secure themselves in this manner, and all otters crush the urchin with their paws prior to scooping out the roe and the viscera with teeth and tongue.

A pair playing frisbee with a hubcap was mentioned earlier. Hunters reported the otters tossing kelp bladders into the air. Most commonly known is the manual dexterity to pound together bivalves or to hammer bivalves against the rock anvil that he often lugs about with him — in readiness. And, Enhydra has been caught red-handed more than once pounding the shell of an abalone underwater to dislodge it. The act of toting about a favorite stone by tucking it under one armpit has many variations. Surplus food items also get tucked into the sagging skin of the chest-armpit area. An otter visiting a United States Fish and Wildlife station in the Aleutians where she was assured of a handout, demonstrated the value of her market basket by stuffing eighteen two-inch clams into the pouch. When number nineteen proved too many, most of the clams then fell to the ground. The greedy freeloader then pressed eight clams to her belly with her forearm, and shuffled off to the sea on three legs. When last seen, she was floating with belly and clams skyward, leisurely dining on her cadged meal.

A captive might pound and chip away at the cement edge of his pool with a rock. The drain in Susie's pool in the Seattle Woodland Park zoo was covered with a fitted wire mesh. The otter removed the mesh so many times that the keepers covered the drain with a sturdier screen, reinforced with a metal band. But Susie continued pounding until this, too, gave way.

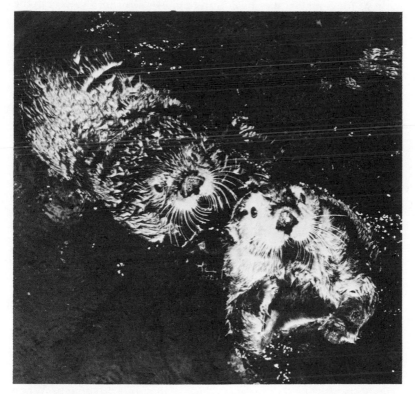

NORTHERN OTTERS exhibited at Seattle Aquarium in 1978. (Seattle Aquarium Photo)

It is the result of the stimuli upon all of Enhydra's senses, motivating emotional or mental processes, which buttresses man's theory that Enhydra's position on the intellectual ladder is well toward the summit. He is the only subprimate mammal for which reliable observations have been made of the use of a tool. Another characteristic of his species which gives weight to the belief that he is most intelligent is the length of the time the offspring remains at home. How long the child's training period lasts in the case of the otter appears one entire year. There is that much to learn before going off to seek his fortune — not that he leaves the pod, but he does become independent of his mother.

The yearling is very likely to be at home even after he has a new sibling, for females may bear pups only in alternate years.

There has not been the opportunity for controlled experiments to test the otter's intelligence, but perhaps these are forthcoming. One measure of intelligence is the degress of readiness with which one can change or adapt from one situation to a new situation. The Russians found their captives quick to adjust, to cope with a new situation in their new habitat, and said that they were endowed with remarkable intellectual capacities.

One of their otters jumped from the wall into the pool while the water was being changed, bumping his head because the water barely covered the pool bottom. Immediately he got out, turned, and with utmost caution let himself down the pool's sloping wall, braking as much as possible with both of his hindlegs.

For a while the Russians' captives were fed inside a specially tailored box which they entered fearlessly, until the day it was used to catch them for weighing-in. Shortly thereafter the otters cautiously felt the box with their paws to check it out and for successive feedings they entered the box only after convincing themselves that the danger no longer existed.

EIGHT

Evolution and Classification

THE SEA OTTER is an aquatic animal that has made a full circle in his evolution. His ancestors, like those of other land animals, originated in the sea and later moved to the land. Now he is back in the sea.

Either thirty million years ago or one hundred million years ago, some land animals returned to the sea and commenced to adapt both structurally and behaviorally to live efficiently in a new environment, water.

The cetaceans, whale, dolphin, porpoise, are streamlined to the point of having no outer ear or surface mammary glands. By now they have almost no hair remaining, although they have remnant arm and finger bones to prove that their ancestors once crawled, walked, or hopped on land. The smooth seal shows a residue of land animal in the form of distinct toes in his flippers.

We live in that era of the sea otter's evolution which finds him handicapped both on land and in the sea. He is so far advanced to the latter that he is awkward in the former.

Compared to the seals, the otters are poorly adapted to fast swimming and long submergence. Because they feed on slow-moving intertidal and subtidal animals, they have not had to develop fast swimming or deep diving skills. Thus far they can survive only in a narrow zone of shallow water. In the north the maximum depth of a food dive is less than two hundred feet, with the average sixty to eighty (10 to 13 fathoms). The southerner browses between five and forty feet (1 to 7 fathoms) but can dive to 120 feet (20 fathoms) for food. One hundred and fifty feet is the deepest the Russians found the otter capable of diving.

From reports out of the north during the last century came the word that a raft of otters was feeding at the depth of three hundred feet (50 fathoms). And another (more easily verified) report came from a commander of a Bering Sea patrol boat during the year 1897. The officer was bitter that the commercial fishing and canning operations by his countrymen had resulted in harassment for the otters and the very defiling of their hauling-out grounds. This had resulted, he said, in the otters remaining out at sea, refusing to haul out for rest or for giving birth as was customary for them. Their habits had been changed to the extent of using a floating raft of kelp as resting sites and as feeding grounds the banks at thirty fathom depths. This, of course, is the otter's diving depth limit: 180 feet.

Speculation on the otter's ancestry includes the theory that both the land and the sea otter descended from a common ancestor. One branch retained the sharp teeth for shearing flesh, while the other branch's teeth developed into crushing tools.

The seagoing branch of the family apparently took a northeasterly direction to the New World by following the Pacific rim until coming to a halt off Lower California. This may have been between two and twelve million years ago.

Evidence exists to indicate that California's interior valley (San Joaquin) was once a bay whose mouth lay in the vicinity of Monterey Bay. Between the sea and this interior bay lay an island in whose shallows dwelled some pinnipeds and a type of otter (says one scientist). This sea otter-of-sorts may have become Enhydra only three million years ago.

That may be speculation, but there is no speculation that the otter is of the *genus* Enhydra, the *family* mustelidae (this includes the river otter, skunk, weasel), and the *order* carnivore.

NINE

Sex and Reproduction

OTTERS are sexually active the year around, probably reaching the peak in the fall of the year. Among the northerners the timing and distribution of births may vary among the colonies, so widely separated are they and with little or no interaction among them. The southerners appear to have the same annual rhythms in respect to mating. Actually, the subject of seasons, timing, conception and birth seems to continue unresolved for the biologist — and little wonder.

Generally mating takes place in the afternoon. Since mornings and late afternoons are devoted to feeding, perhaps siesta time is the ideal time of day for romance. After finding a female, the male rubs and pets the female's chest, belly, and genital region with his forepaws. If she is receptive, the two nuzzle and fondle each other. In the wild, during the racing and chasing of the foreplay, the female may change course abruptly. Or, she may hide among the rocks briefly.

Finally, according to Dr. Kenyon[4], when the female is ready for copulation, the male approaches her from the rear (differing from the Russian description), and as they copulate the couple move in a circle, rolling as they progress. The male grasps the upper jaw of his mate, presumably for stabilization purposes, very often leaving her with a lacerated nose. Doubtless the female can thank the blunted canines that nature provided, for getting off so easily, although she will sport a raw, pink nose for some time to come.

However, this must be a minor irritation compared with the effort merely to breathe often enough to keep alive. One would conclude from the resulting gasping, shrieking, ducking, and bobbing, that the otter is far from ready to assume marine life in toto. Also, that this perilous procedure would decrease the population; not increase it.

In the north the copulating consumes as much as an hour, during which time the female gradually is moving the couple toward her choice of a hauling-out rock. This will be the pair's trysting place for their two or three days of courtship. Copulation in the south has not been clearly established, but must be done wholly in the sea.

As the couple feed and play together, then rest, groom, sleep, now and then they repeat copulation. On some occasions the female initiates the petting. During the courtship interlude neither lets his mate out of sight, but once the male begins to lose interest, it may extend to the degree of stealing some of his lady's food.

But this breakup can be accomplished by the female as well as the male. When her interest wanes she begins to keep a close surveillance on her mate in preparation for her escape from him. Since it is necessary for the male to eat more and to eat more frequently than the female, she has the opportunity to slip from the trysting place and swim in the opposite direction from the male's destination. Sometimes he searches for his lost partner both by exploring the rocks and by raising himself high in the sea to cast about for signs of his lover.

Some observers believe that the otter mates for life. Perhaps this was a result of comparing his behavior with that of man in such respects as devotion to young, intelligence, invention, individuality. It is indeed difficult to refrain from anthropomorphizing as one observes the extraordinary behavior of Enhydra.

The Russians believed the male plays a feeble role in protecting the family, but American observers disagree, having seen possessive mothers chase away curious males approaching their young pup. No one knows whether or not the male was showing interest in what he considered his family.

A female matures at three or four years of age; at least the northern lutris does so. In the north the pupping season appears to peak during spring and early summer. In the south, late winter and early spring. Gestation period is twelve or thirteen months with roughly half of that time in implantation phase.

In the north the pups may be born in the sea or on the shingle or rocks of the shore. In the south, in the sea, although it is unwise to make so definitive a statement, for otters have been returning to shore for brief visits since 1971 in the Monterey Bay vicinity.

How a creature is born, head first or feet (tail) first, reveals much about his species. Since a whale calf a-borning must make his way with all dispatch to the surface and break it to reach the oxygen supply, he is better off tail-first, presumably. To be born head first does not seem nature's way, for the calf's breathing apparatus would be that much longer underwater.

Given the halfway point at which the otter (especially the northerner) stands in his evolution seaward, it seems predictable that his presentation at birth be head or tail in the proportion of fifty percent of the births.

The southerner's presentation remains a mystery, although it is certain that its pups have been born in the sea for many a generation. One could hazard a guess as approximately a century, or since the human harassment increased to an intolerable degree, pushing him out beyond the breaker line, bag and baggage.

It seems safe to say that pups are born in alternate years; that they remain with their mother as apprentices for a year. They are likely to be with her when their baby brother or sister is born, and even afterward. Twin births are highly unlikely. Biologists have assumed that a female will not be receptive to a male until her pup is about a year of age and ready to fledge. But the 1978 research made by the California Department of Fish and Game discovered a female accepting a male while still engaged in parenting an unweaned pup.

Also, mating can occur soon after the death of a young pup, thus changing the two-year cycle.

In captivity: little information on observations of mating and giving birth is available. The most practical mix of genders for a contented community in captivity was discovered by the directors of the aquarium at Pt. Defiance, Tacoma: one male to several females. The lucky male was Gus.

But a far greater problem has arisen since this early-1970s decision: none of the pups fathered by Gus lived beyond the forty-seventh day. Some may have been premature births, but could all of them have been? How to avoid this tragedy remains a conundrum. To remove the pregnant female does not seem the solution because of the gregarious character of the species. So vital is this factor that Sea World veterinarians believe it therapeutic to introduce an ailing otter into their otter community. They have practiced this successfully at Sea World.

One of the most likely explanations considered for the early infant deaths at Pt. Defiance is one that the directors are reluctant to embrace: that in captivity the male and father killed the newborns by drowning them.

TEN

Emotions, Temperament, Individuality

LITTLE by little biologists, zoologists, and veterinarians have been learning how to treat Enhydra in the process of capture, holding, and maintaining his health to prolong his life under the exotic circumstances of captivity. With the mechanics of these procedures improving, the successes have been multiplying by leaps and bounds.

The problems to overcome have not been simply the fundamental mechanics for sparing Enhydra bodily grief; his emotions are involved, also. Even individual temperament seems to demand consideration (this is not to imply that other species do not have individuality as well).

Clearly the otter has deep need for communication with his own species. The Russians concluded that he tolerated loneliness so poorly that his appetite diminished when he was deprived of the company of his own kind. (That does manifest a grave condition!)

Clearly Enhydra needs an occupation. The otter is a forager or or browser. (Recently a young biologist suggests that Enhydra be called a browser or grazer, since he does not stalk or hunt food.) A captive, with time on his paws, deprived of his browsing occupation must do something besides eat, sleep, groom. (Considering his rugged individualism could it be sufficient for some?)

The expensive otterarium built in 1969 at Pt. Defiance, Tacoma, Washington, with the expert counsel of the otter authorities of the United States Department of Fish and Wildlife (Sports Fisheries), was the last word in comfort and safety for its lodgers. It was a pair of pools connected by a passage or canal, and the water was constantly changing seawater. The walls were glass and brick and entirely roofed to discourage the tossing of foreign objects into the habitat. In a word, it promised the most nearly perfect environment for captives as yet provided.

A year or so after the opening of the habitat, the racket from some construction work near, but not in, the otterarium's locality distressed the otters. Their concerned guardians surmised that if the captives could *see* the activity, it might not upset them. Since this was out of the question, the alternative was to let the otters see what was transpiring immediately outside their home.

Modifications in the habitat were made: shutters removed from the windows of the main pool and only the windows of the smaller pool left covered. The scheme was to give the mammals the small one for retreating when they wanted quiet or privacy.

Once the changes were made, the otters began to spend ninety percent of the waking hours in the main pool, the one giving them a view of the passing parade of human activity.

In the wild, along the California coast, otters occasionally rise head and shoulders from the sea to peer curiously at humans on the shore. During the 1970s, visitors to, and residents of, beaches and bluffs reported instances of otter inquisitiveness.

Individual mammals of the southern pioneering front approached the shore as close as the breaker line to stare at children and adults. Two different otters moved parallel to the strand as the humans strolled along, turned, and strolled back. On many occasions one otter drew nearer to land when a woman donned her red sweater and paced the bluff on which her home stood.

In 1978 the equivalent of the pacing of a caged lion or tiger appeared in the between-feeding routine of the three females and one male in Seattle's magnificent new aquarium. The male, whose theoretical territory comprises almost half of the pool, repeatedly swam in an established triangular route. At an angle and as far as possible, he swam on his back toying with an empty clamshell. Then he dived, turning to swim on his belly (and continuing to carry the shell).

Two of the females wore a veritable groove in the other half of the pool: at an angle, also, as though to get the most mileage in their allotted space. At regular intervals they would break their sprints with a bout of play. The third female merely dived in one spot; always the same spot. Then she would bob to the surface, touch her left cheek with her left paw, and plummet straight down once again!

Chow call interrupted these routines now and then. Also the two playgirls occasionally swam below to emerge through the port in the cement platform running the length of their two-story deep pool. Perhaps this served for variety to break the monotony of their routine.

Dr. Kenyon[4] reported Seattle's Susie's routine swimming pattern. He called it an exercise routine.

What is the explanation of Susie's dogged determination to work over the drain in her pool with a rock? Frustration resulting from boredom resulting from lack of occupation? She also beat the edge of her pool with a stone. It is Dr. Kenyon's theory that an otter's shattering mollusk against mollusk or mollusk against stone anvil, is frustration — also the basis for Susie's hobby.

Because this shell fracturing is a practice of the southern otter, *E. lutris nereis*, many tend to believe it a practice among all otters. However, the mollusks available to the northern, *E. lutris lutris*, are mussels. And these are smaller than the mussels of Washington, Oregon, and California. Hence they can be crushed with the post-canines. There are no hard-shelled clams in the northerner's habitat, hence he has no need for the anvil tool.

However, when captive Aleutian otters were first offered clams they did shatter them against a rock, against another clam on their chest, or against the wall of the habitat. Moreover, a female that rejected a smelt and some herrings attacked the edge of the pool with them. Off Amchitka Dr. Kenyon watched two subadult otters pounding one chunk of coralline algae against another chunk as it lay on their chest. He believed this to be play since the mammals did not search the broken fragments for edible organisms.

According to this biologist, chest-pounding with the forepaws commonly occurs among the northern otters as a result of being robbed of food by another otter. He believes that the pounding is expressing frustration and that even the practice of pounding two

STONE ANVIL in use by a dining otter in Aleutian Islands. (Karl W. Kenyon Photo, Bureau of Sport Fisheries & Wildlife)

organisms together may originate in the frustration of failing to open them with the teeth.

Dr. Kenyon is not the only biologist who believes that the pounding behavior is not a deliberately devised skill, as it is with man and his tools. He compares it with the seagull's use of gravity as a tool: by dropping a bivalve from aloft to the wet beach sand the shell is shattered for him.

He believes that the use of the rock anvil is but a "behavioral adaptation" without special relevance to the "evolution of the sort of intelligent, anticipatory" skills "most highly developed in man and which he uses" for the manufacture of a standard set of tools to be kept for use.[4]

One wonders, however, if those who do not deem the anvil as a "devised anticipatory skill" remember that the southern otter commonly lugs the rock tool with him in his foraging travels. Wouldn't this custom be classified under "anticipation"?

But, what matters the motivation for invention: necessity, frustration, or another incentive? The fact remains that something moves the brain to move the paw or the claw to employ an object as instrument necessary for accomplishing a means to an end.

As pacifistic as the otters may be, the trait of aggressiveness dwells in all or some of them, emerging both in captivity and in the wild as food-stealing.

Among those otters of the southern migrating front a little drama played out between a young adult male and a mature one resting close by him. Three times the younger surfaced with a shellfish, only to have it ripped off by the senior. Finally the younger moved from the scene, dived, and brought up a fourth item, only to have it confiscated by another foraging male.

This time the younger male put up a struggle and succeeded in keeping prize number five!

Biologists point out that this is an indication of an established social hierarchy of an otter community. It may explain in part why the rafting otters scatter when it is foraging time.

Dr. Kenyon has seen males, repulsed by an unreceptive female, snatch whatever food items she was holding on her chest, and make off with them. He has seen Amchitka otters rob one another during seasons of extreme shortage of food, but humans can understand this more easily than the robbing under the other circumstances.

In captivity much robbing occurs. Customarily the adults of the little family of the Woodland Park zoo in Seattle (during the 1960s) robbed smaller adults and juveniles, even when the aggressors already had filled their pouches. They would approach their victim from the rear or from beneath, and with one or both paws wrench the food items from the victim's chest. Dr. Kenyon reports that certain females growled and snapped at a male robber, but put up no resistance. They merely rolled away from the thief and put some distance between themselves and him.

Here, too, the victim might show anger or frustration by beating the chest.

To reduce this pilferage at Woodland Park, attendants used a bamboo pole to discourage the robbers. But one adult female was so clever that she could dive and at the same time reach with one foreleg above the surface to snatch the food from the chest of a large juvenile that was floating and eating.

She mended her ways — at least in the presence of the attendants.

During courtship male otters exhibit little territorial aggressiveness, as far as is known. A few males have been observed protecting a little cove where their trysting was in progress, by chasing off an intruding male — or a male just passing by. The trespasser left peaceably and without altercation.

Juveniles will frolic, playing their version of follow-the-leader, repeatedly surfacing from below to bounce on the belly of a dozing senior. The youngsters may do this until their mother calls them to heel, but the senior will tolerate the nuisance without as much as snapping or boxing the kids' ears.

ELEVEN

Thermoregulation

CHANCES are that those who have heard of the unique sea otter are aware of his strange mode of regulating body temperature. It is up to him to maintain his own insulation against the water and the air by keeping his pelage dry. Its fur fibers must be maintained as a honeycomb of airpockets, like the fiberglass wadding used for insulating buildings. Only the otter himself can build and sustain this condition; that is, after he learns to assume this demanding task from his mother.

To make a living, creatures below man on the fauna ladder continuously move about in the most cautious manner, for they have predators continuously moving about stalking them. And others stalk those stalkers, *ad inf*. One wonders if there are other wild animals blessed with the sea otter's conditions, so predator-free. Not entirely free, but relatively free.

Enhydra's thermoregulation system is the story of his adaptation to the sea as his evolution prepared him for this colossal transition from land to sea. Perhaps Enhydra could move into the aquatic ambience because in it he had few natural enemies. (We shall forget man, who forced him into the great transition earlier than may have been nature's plan). Had he enemies, predators, stalking him like other animals of water, land, or air, he would be deprived of the time necessary for 1) keeping his skin dry and 2) hunting so great a quantity of food necessary to maintain his body heat.

If the sea otter appears nervous, jumpy, hyperactive, even bolting his food, it may be the result of living in this alien situation wherein he is occupied almost constantly with activities necessary for his grooming. He does not gulp his food in his haste to move to a safer place to do his digesting.

One of the costs of going aquatic is that he must be up and at it again and again, grooming his fur by squeezing water from it, by replenishing its airpockets, rustling up food, and so on and on. Until a few years ago observers believed that his diving, rolling, wheeling, porpoising, was play. Now it appears that much of this business falls under grooming for purposes of staying alive.

From the first transplants (during the 1960s in the Aleutians under the supervision of the Department of the Interior's Fish and Wildlife Service) came the earliest lessons in the consequences of depriving Enhydra of water, clean water, under captive circumstances. Because of man's ignorance of the otter's needs, he caused many fatalities. Rapid transit, he soon learned, was of prime importance, with cleanliness running a close second. Airplanes replaced boats, then jet planes replaced prop planes, and with this the chances for successfully translocating otters grew in leaps and bounds.

First, in an attempt to transplant a few Aleutian otters by boat to reestablish them in islands of the northern waters formerly inhabited by their species, they were kept in captivity for eight days prior to transplantation. When they were re-introduced into the sea, in less than one minute after hitting the water they were screaming from the chill. One female returned to the dory, was pulled aboard, and was unconscious within twenty minutes. The frigid water had penetrated her fur to the skin. The pelage was matted from becoming soiled, lying on dry bedding without opportunity to bathe and to recover the fur's necessary condition.

Paradoxically the otter can live in water as far north as the region of pack ice. He can lie on snow throughout the night during the harshest of winters. He has lived as far north as ten degrees above the Pribilovs, or at sixty-four degrees north latitude.

And yet the Russian experimenters learned that the otters are subject to colds. They transferred some from the Commander Islands

(55°N) to Murmansk (about 68°N) where most of them perished from inflammation of the lungs.

Thermoregulating Enhydra's system includes more than the process of retaining or recovering body heat, and retarding the invasion of cold. From heating-up following feeding, mating, or other caloric squandering, doubtless the otter must cool down. His fluffing of his fur as he commences yet another grooming session must help to release heat from body to atmosphere, as it does for a bird. Or for a overheated dog, stretching his full length to separate the fur fibers as much as possible and to allow the air to circulate among them.

The broad, webbed flippers release body heat by expansion, and perhaps by raising and lowering them from and to the water.

Was it Darwin who said that an animal cannot change its situation?

Years and years hence, after nature has provided Enhydra with blubber tissue, he should be able to relax more frequently and work less frequently by decreasing his caloric intake. However, since nature abhors a vacuum, doubtless other circumstances will intervene to occupy the time he now uses for foraging and grooming.

At present, his manifold daily duties include fluffing the fur, blowing air into it to replenish the airpockets, squeezing moisture from the pelage, and keeping head and paws and flippers out of the sea as frequently as possible. Underwater films show Enhydra's leaving a wake of silvery bubbles as his fur loses a measure of that air — only one means of shedding the laboriously-constructed insulation.

While belly up, the otter squeezes his fur with his forepaws from time to time to remove the water, then licks up this moisture. He reaches between his legs, grasps the lumbar fur, and pulls it forward to the surface for aerating that region. The dorsal's underfur, being the thickest, longest, and best insulated, needs the least attention. A twitch from time to time seems sufficient for its maintenance.

The Russians think the otter's occupation also includes massaging to stimulate the skin's oil for lubricating the fur. The biologists of San Diego's Sea World aquarium, host to a number of California otters since the early 1970s, claim that chlorinated water tended to remove the natural oils from the fur of one of their pups whom they lost. Her coat became badly matted, losing much of its insulating quality. (Within six months the pup was dead, but with other complications.)

Since a pup must spend close to a year in training before stepping out in the world to make his own living, obviously the mere grooming process takes an apprenticeship. Could it be that this Sea World orphan was unable to maintain her pelage because her mother had done it up to the time she rolled onto the beach that stormy day? Her human friends attempted to groom her as surrogate mothers, but in vain; apparently it takes an otter to groom an otter.

As an experiment the Russians clipped a sample of fur from one of their captives. Thereafter the deprived animal continually scratched at the site in an attempt to cover and to reinsulate it. The otter's principal threat is soiled fur, allowing the separation of the fibers which in turn allows water to reach the flesh. Chill, pneumonia, death, are almost certain to follow.

To consider rescuing an otter oilstained from a tanker spill may be a pipedream, although 1977 brought a welcome investigation into the means of rescuing an otter from such an eventuality. Researchers believe that using a type of gillnet is the most promising, plus those anesthetics proved to be appropriate for the otter. Relatively few pelagic birds have survived cleansing, and they are small and docile compared with the independent and feisty otter. Sadly enough, both the northern and the southern otters live on the shipping lanes plied daily by oil tankers and their big brothers, the supertankers.

The prime concern of the Department of Fish and Game of Alaska is that the accelerated oil and gas development might adversely affect their otters, now numbering between one hundred thousand and one hundred and forty thousand.

So much for the importance of keeping the body as warm and as dry as possible. Another danger for Enhydra is heat stress. When out of sea or pool he is in jeopardy if his body cannot be cooled frequently, as is the case with his cousin, the river otter. Perhaps no table of frequency of bathing rules exists, but both Russian biologists and their American counterparts have had experience with so vital a need as this one. Laymen, also.

That the otter must not be left beyond reach of water for more

than a hour would seem an acceptable rule of thumb, according to
the Russians. And they mean at any time of the year, at least in
Murmansk and the Commander Islands. From an American's point
of view these locales would never be warm, but during their summer the captives had to be returned to the pool after five or ten minutes out of it. If not, manifestations of heat stroke appeared: rapid
and powerful pulse, trembling body, eyes bloodshot, heavy panting
through wide-open mouth. One heatstroke victim was so enfeebled
that he reached the water with difficulty and frequently collapsed
enroute to the pool.

In what the Russians called "hot" weather, the otters went into
convulsions during the weighing-in, a brief and painless operation.
The captors were not certain, however, whether this resulted from
the experience of the weighing or from the heat proper.

Their captives spent almost the entire summer in the pool. Unfortunately, only one summer was given the Russians for experimentation, for a war intervened to bring the project to a halt.

Someone brought to the Department of Fish and Game office of
a California coastal town a two-week old pup that had rolled ashore
and was found crying on the beach. The Department officer took it
to a small, privately-owned aquarium used as an official distress
station and one with a splendid record for maintaining marine fauna.
The biologists knew that the odds against the pup's survival were
great, so had little hope for it. And yet, it lived a contented, healthy
three months before its demise.

For this pup, physical and emotional conditions were close to
ideal. The adoptive parents loved her, fed her perfectly, and gave
her an ideal situation throughout the day in their aquarium, and
another one during the night in their home.

The babe had small and large tanks in which to bathe, and within
days after her arrival was signalling her parents when she was ready
for a dip, night or day. Just prior to the dip her body would be considerably warmer than usual to the parents' touch, but it was the
pup's particular cry that warned of her need for a cooling-down.

An unexpectedly warm couple of days and nights struck the beach
town in July. Simultaneously, a pair of crises struck the couple's
staff and family. The distraction by these, the unusual weather, and

the misunderstanding of the pup's cries during the fatal night, all combined to result in the pup's death from heat stress.

During warm days the pup's thirst was far greater than normal, which in restrospect indicates a possible illness. Also, the pup may have been a runt, or a premie, for it was especially small. The majority of those normal pups given or loaned to San Diego's Sea World failed to survive, and the conditions must have been superior, for the adults living there have survived for several years in the best of health.

It would be gratifying if such a problem could be solved as was the one in a cove of Monterey Bay. A storm tossed this babe ashore and nearby residents heard its cries. Although they searched for the mother, they failed to find her, so carried the pup home. They asked the advice of a biologist or veterinarian to learn what to feed the visitor, then gave it a formula of whipping cream and babyfood.

After a night's rest in a sleeping bag with the young boy of the family, help came in the form of a pair of experienced scuba divers. The following morning, with the surf continuing rough, the men lashed a wire basket to their surfboard, placed the pup in it, and slid out to the edge of the kelp forest.

Here they deposited the babe on a thick snarl of kelp, then back-paddled some distance to watch until they saw the mother sprint toward her offspring for a happy ending.

That was a case of a fortunate pup, as well as fortunate humans.

SECTION THREE
THE OTTER'S PAST

TWELVE
Three Centuries In The Old World

NATURALLY Americans are more aware of the Great Hunt in the New World, their hemisphere. But, actually the range of fur mammals reached from the Americas to Northern Japan, and man besieged the sea otter and the fur seal its entire length.

The Ainu people of northern Japan hunted otter initially off their own shores, selling the pelts to Japanese feudal lords. Many of these furs found their way to China. In 1633 the Ainus began to hop over to the southern Kurile Islands to hunt the eagle, bear, and otter. Here they found competition: Russian hunters with firearms. Again, northern China was the destination for the finest of their furs.

By the early 1700s the Russians had invaded the Kuriles, and in 1795 The Russian American Fur Company established a headquarters there. Transplanted Aleuts and Kamchatkans did the harvesting. Evidently there were otters in untold quantities thriving in that climate, a climate which had to surpass in gray, clammy bleakness any locale that the otter had yet called home. From the literature it appears to surpass the Aleutians with their 125 mph winds and 50- and 75-foot seas.

The Japanese sent some eager pioneers to settle in the south of the Kuriles late in the 1800s, following Russia's cession of the island chain in exchange for lower Sakhalin. But life must have been so darkly depressing for these voluntary exiles that they simply lay down and expired, their bodies to be found by passersby exploring their island home. H. J. Snow[3], the British fur hunter, called the cause of this communal perishing "inanition", which the Britannica defines as "the state of being void or empty". (Perhaps no spot on the planet is without total charm for some of its creatures: the otter vibrated to the region... and eagles and bears... In any case, the mass suicide may have been a reprieve for the otter, the single positive event in his history between 1600 and 1911.)

After the Kurile Islands became a Japanese possession, Japan patrolled the waters of the islands to discourage the Russian poachers, but the poachers would simply sail a few miles beyond the three-mile limit and return to hunt later. And like them, the otters also grew cagey, swimming five or six miles to sea to lie up for the day. They would return to shore at night or during stormy weather to do their foraging.

According to hunter Snow, he himself removed a thousand pelts between 1873 and 1895 from these forested isles running north of Japan toward the Kamchatka peninsula to separate the North Pacific Ocean from the Sea of Okhotsk. Snow claims that his pelts were from the last of the colonies of the chain, and yet there had to be residue enough to maintain the species there. The Russians were observing otters there during the 1960s, having regained possession of the Kuriles following World War II.

In any case, the opportunity to effect any conservation of the resource at this extreme of the otter range was lost, just as it was in the balance of the otter habitat.

THIRTEEN
Shift To The New World

THE GREAT HUNT in the New World, a drama stretching from 1741 to almost 1900, meant bitter years for the otter, but far, far more so for all of the natives of the Aleutian Islands and many of those of the mainland.

Tsar Peter the Great, curious as to whether or not the American continent was joined to his continent, hired the Dane, Vitus Bering, to make an exploration to determine this once and for all. Shipwrecked on one of what were to be named the Commander Islands (less than two hundred miles west of the tip of the Aleutian chain), Bering and his men found a mammal unknown to them inhabiting its shores and shallows. The starving men easily caught the friendly and curious mammal, ate its flesh, then used its coat to keep themselves from freezing.

It is strange that the totality of the crew could be ignorant of the mammal that the Russians called *kalan*. Not only had Russian hunters and traders dealt in the pelts of the cousins of Enhydra inhabiting the Kurile Islands, but the Kamchatka Peninsula south of Siberia had been its habitat for many, many years.

Bering died on the island before his men succeeded in assembling a makeshift vessel for their return home. But Georg Steller, the German naturalist accompanying the expedition, had time and opportunity to make sketches and to record his observations of the otter's unusual behavior. And, on its return to Asia the crew found the fabulous otter fur demand and market for the few otter pelts they had brought home with them from their island.

This touched·off the stampede to the Aleutians.

Siberia had a class of hunters, untamed and long-accustomed, hardened, to a harsh mode of life: the *Promyshlenniki,*or Proms, some of which were Russian exiles. Many joined the fur rush, and in their haste to sail many went down with their jurybuilt vessels. Dubbed *shitiki* (sewed or stitched) these hastily constructed craft were easily swamped, made as they were of unseasoned timbers no more than lashed together with leather thongs.

The Proms had been hunting otter and fur seal in the Aleutians some forty years before the Russian and Siberian fur companies established factories there and hired some of them as hunters. On their arrival the invaders found the inhabitants of the Aleutians, as some described them, a cheerful and vigorous race numbering thirty thousand souls. For many succeeding generations of these stone-age aborigines the Great Hunt was to constitute more than a terror-filled span of years. As a result of the greedy, fierce dedication of the Siberians plus the representatives of a half-dozen other nations, the ravishing of their homelands for pelts of fox and sea mammals soon brought their race to the border of genocide.

Harold McCracken[5], marooned in 1917 among descendants of this once independent and harmless people, listened for many months to the reminiscences of the oldtimers. Their narratives, long since indelibilized, had been bequeathed them by one generation to the next since the advent of the fur rush in a remote and unspoiled corner of the New World.

Genocide: it was accomplished by murder, by introduced disease, and by dilution. The Aleuts were first degraded, then destroyed. McCracken said that the story of the century of rule under the Russians is "a saga of one of primitive man's most ruthless eras of humam subjugation, cruelty, and rapine in frontier history."

The Tsar hired the German physician and naturalist Georg von Langsdorff[6] to participate in the Russian voyage-of-discovery of 1803. His account is a rich source of information on the times and the personalities involved in the sea otter hunt and habitats. Over a

NORTHERN PUPS with Alaska native friend are unaware of the Great Hunt in their heritage. (Karl W. Kenyon Photo, Bureau of Sport Fisheries and Wildlife)

period of at least two years von Langsdorff visited the otter territory of the Pacific shores between California and Siberia.

During the medico's several months on Kamchatka in 1806 he learned that the otter was first found on that peninsula, but had already been extirpated. Here they called the mammal the *Kamschadale biber* (beaver).

According to von Langsdorff the hierarchy of the Russian or Siberian fur companies in the field was headed by the superintendent or director of either one factory or a chain of them. Beneath him was the manager or overseer of a single factory, and beneath him, the under-overseer. Apparently the latter held the Proms both in thrall and in debt, and almost as subjugated as the natives. According to von Langsdorff these were a mixed bag: some cruel and others humane. One under-overseer he described as exceeding all belief in the abuse and repression of his Proms.

The Proms were between the under-overseer and the native hunters, it would seem, and became not only enslaved but exploited as expendable, disposable, laborers. The physican compared this system to that of the black slave system he had seen in his world travels, in which it was to the black's master's advantage to keep well and healthy the laboring chattels in whom he had a cash investment. Not so (said von Langsdorff) in the case of the Aleut. He was used to pull plows to cultivate the potato and barley fields, and his women, who were shipped between island factories on order like measures of flour or casks of molasses and brandy, did everything but the hunting.

The procedure for what the doctor called the depopulation of the Aleutian race, included forcing the healthy males on hunting treks for months, even years, at a time. Seldom did any of them return to the bosom of their families.

In 1806 the physician visited some villages to find only superannuated, female, and child residents — no males capable of labor. One village had had a population of a thousand, but by the time he visited, it had but forty. He found Kodiak (one of the larger islands and headquarters of the Russian American Fur Company), with no males able to hunt or to work.

Von Langsdorff gave as the principal cause of the depopulation the extensive overseas hunting sorties in the native cockleshell baidarkas, the two-man kayak which he considered man's greatest discovery. These forays, he said, resulted in the inflammation of the lungs, eventually fatal. Also contributing were the oppression and the total lack of care. (The Proms' state of misery was identical, of course: if they sickened they received no attention, either.) And finally, the enforced changes in the natives' customs and mores made their contribution to the downfall of the "Americans" (as the doctor called them, and correctly so).

Von Langsdorff made no mention of the effect of firewater on the aborigines, but other observers have recited the devastation that its introduction wrought upon the Aleuts. It was the old and familiar story: under the addiction they might eventually agree to trade for a bottle what property was not already in the foreigner's hands: a member of the family.

One tribe, at least, rejected brandy and rum: the mainland Tlingits and their subtribe, the Sitkas.

Von Langsdorff depicted the Russians and Siberians as criminals, malefactors, and adventurers completely devoid of honor or principal. He reported that the original manager of the Russian American Fur Company (which settled originally in the Aleutians, moving east as the furs grew scarce, until establishing a factory on the mainland) reduced the estimated 25,000 population of Kodiak and adjacent isles to 6500 in 1795, and to less than 5000 by 1804. Unalaska Island's male population in 1783 numbered in the thousands, but fell to 1300 by 1790 and to 300 by 1804.

During the voyage-of-discovery of the English explorer Vancouver to the fur fields in the early 1780s he witnessed the departure of a flotilla of 700 baidarkas and 1400 hunters. According to von Langsdorff, by 1805 the Russian American Fur Company could not muster as many as 400 baidarkas. Of 140 canoes and 280 Aleuts sent to sea in November (winter!) of 1805, only thirty baidarkas with their sixty hunters made their way back to port.

The status and condition of the Proms was all but identical to that of the natives, with the overseers and the under-overseers using some as laborers whether ill, starving, or scurvy-ridden, and placing others in charge of the Aleuts.

These Proms perforce underwent the same rigors and punishment of the hunt as the Aleuts did. For example, during the long and unrelieved sea journeys, when no camp or cooking fires were allowed during the rest stops for fear of spooking the quarry, the suffering and discomfort were not selective.

It was common for the Proms to live among the Aleuts and adopt their mode of life, coarse and mean as it was. Yet, despite their state of oppression a measure of gratification or reward, plus power and force, was theirs. They held sway over another stratum of humans, and they had all the harems they desired, plus complete absence of responsibility. Von Langsdorff was astonished to hear that when the company's inspector, Nicolai Rezanov, attempted to sack a number of Proms because of the severely reduced production of furs, some fell on their knees to beg him to retain them. They did not relish returning to Siberia.

TREADING WATER in a kelp canopy, curious otter stands high to gape at humans. For one year a wandering male swam daily with human friends at Malibu shore. (Paul Wild Photo, DFG)

Why did the Aleut not revolt? A score of years after Bering revealed the otter wealth of our Pacific northwest a minor revolt among the native hunter-slaves did erupt. Whoever was in charge of them ordered a dozen of the offenders bound together with a rope and shot at close range in an experiment to determine whether an average power charge could send a ball through twelve bodies. It couldn't; only nine of the men lost their lives.

Holding hostages was another successful means to force the Aleut hunter to meet a quota of furs. Punishment might take the form of roping together several women, then throwing them into the sea. Removing the natives' means of livelihood by confiscating baidarkas, harpoon tips, even clothing, was a common and foolproof means to help reduce the Aleut to helplessness.

In the process of breaking their spirit, the supreme persuader was the musket with its magic musketball, which the simple people believed followed them no matter in which direction or how fleet they might run to escape it. The hunt was thirty or forty years along before it was possible for the natives to play with firearms. It was when the rivalry in the field intensified that white hunters, traders, and companies began issuing the natives guns to use to the advantage of the whites themselves. Apparently it was the Yankees that first used this item of trade among their other schemes to ultimately fleece someone of peltry. Even the women were hunting with firearms by the turn of the century; presumably for themselves, however.

The treatment of the natives changed to a degree with the arrival on the scene of organized fur companies. Even the attention of the Tsarina Catherine the Great was called to the cruelty and she was compelled to warn the companies against inhumane exploitation.

But the pardon came too late; thousands and thousands of natives too late.

In any case, we must not condemn the Siberians alone. Surely they had no corner on cruelty or want of self-discipline in those long dark days of exploration and expansion, the free-for-all, the 54,40, or Fight, era. Nor in more recent times. Nor today. How many nations or tribes have or have had a record free of instances of inhumanity toward their fellows? Any one that has resisted the temptation (like our unique southwest Hopi tribe) to exploit another one must serve as the exception to the human species.

As late as the final days of the 1800s Yankees in northern California held hunting forays to kill Indians and to drive them into the mountain wildernesses which the whites had as yet no designs upon. In some instances the army joined the local vigilante pack, with genocide their overt objective. The Yankee argonauts invading the California Mother Lode during the Gold Rush ran to the ground many of their Mexican counterparts. Again the objective was sometimes to dislodge this (excellent) competition or to exterminate the miners on the spot. Their mining skills were the Mexicans' doom; their mining skills were a threat to the Yankee's amateur standing.

In restrospect, perhaps we should redefine the term *savage*, for it has come to connote hostility and aggression instead of simple and uncivilized. Which were the savages of the Great Hunt: the unconquered or the conquered?

FOURTEEN

Enter Baranov

ALEKSANDR ANDREYEVICH BARANOV, the most glamorous, despised, and respected actor treading the boards of the northeastern Pacific stage through its historic drama of the Great Otter and Fur Seal Hunt. The little man's courage, some said, was the only stock in trade he had brought with him from Siberia in 1790 to manage the Russian American Fur Company the succeeding thirty years.

Our literature describes this man with a mix of terms both admiring and condemning: despotic, brutal, a leader of men, respected, invincible, unscrupulous, original, dreaded, ruthless slavedriver without regard for human life, deceitful, remarkable, irresistible, indomitable, and a master salesman. Our own Washington Irving credited Baranov's persuasive success to punch and peltries, for he was a royal host, and a hard drinker whom no guest was known to outdrink.

Many a ship's captain and his officers contributed to this lexicon depicting Baranov's character and modus operandi. He entertained droves of traders who sought the company of a man quickly renowned via the grapevine in the shipping and trading world. At the height of Baranov's ironfisted rule, the rum and brandy ran as freely as the song from his choral groups at the parties he gave for these visitors from Europe and the young United States of America.

Baranov entered rather late in the Great Hunt to find the otter population already well eroded and the competition tempting hunters and hunting companies to employ desperate means to secure pelts. It was he who had the corner on unscrupulous methods whereby he maintained the flow of dividends to his company's shareholders. Apparently he cared little for material wealth for himself, retiring with few rubles to his name, plus a modest bit of stock in the firm. He strove for his company and its stockholders.

According to von Langsdorff[6], Baranov always was carrying some project for the general good (what "general" means is unclear, but the doctor did view the world through rose-colored glasses at times). Baranov cared little for creature comforts, either; as long as he had an ample supply of firewater, it appears that he could live under primitive conditions almost equalling those of his Proms. Eventually he reached a flush period, to live in regal style — for a frontier.

For the most part of his career at Sitka and Kodiak, Baranov was forced to cope and to cope again, because the promised supply line between the Siberian headquarters and his stations was either nonexistent or unreliable. However, making do Baranov took in stride. Someone visited him during a rainstorm, at a point in his experience in which he lived in a hovel. Seeing Baranov's bed afloat the visitor asked if the water was entering where a board was missing. The manager replied, "No, it's the same old leak."

Baranov's Proms, who had both fear and esteem for him, lived the miserable life of a native: close to the earth, dirty, without any comforts-of-home because they hadn't them when they were home. Their new lifestyle must have demanded but minor adjustment; the Proms had been living on the bedrock, subsistence, hand to mouth, level back in Siberia. The improvements their new life did grant them was a measure of power over other men, making them little kings themselves: the natives did most of the grubbing labor of the hunting and the Proms had autonomy over them.

Incidents renewing the Proms' respect for and faith in the manager must have arisen frequently. When battling the Indians, Baranov refused to leave the frontlines, even when injured. On an occasion in which he had a seagoing vessel of his own (once he had one built by scratching and scraping from close to nothing by way of materials, and he drove the Proms to do the work) he and his men were caught in a storm at sea. Seeing this threatening his five hundred Aleuts and their baidarkas who were accompanying the ship, Baranov ordered his personal baidarka lowered to the sea so that he could accompany the natives.

He must have been what some described: an iron man. Anyone who transformed disasters into successes would have to be a leader, and his entire reign in the northwest was confrontation with one disaster after another. At the nadir of his managerial career Baranov's meld of luck and cunning brought him his most profitable year of all thirty in the wilderness.

By 1802 the Russian American Fur Company with its imperial charter now in its fist, was to all intents and purposes the arm of the Russian government throughout the hunting grounds. Yet, long before the company was granted the favor of monopoly Baranov had been intimidating his compatriot competitors to convince them that his company already had the charter-granted priority, and that *he* was the Russian American Fur Company

The year 1802 saw some of the beleaguered natives sufficiently angry and confident to turn on Baranov's men, then turn to kill some of his slavelabor force of Aleuts. These were the Tlingits and Sitkas, tribes which never yielded to the invaders (neither did they yield to liquor). There appears much evidence that the massacre of Sitka (then called New Arcangel) was not solely the natives' venture, but that they were in collusion with visiting Yankee and English captains and crews. The resulting massacre of the Sitka settlement offered Baranov yet another opportunity to exhibit his ingenuity and invincibility. He did not surrender, but rebuilt the station — plus another one. He merely retreated, regrouped, and returned.

In describing this effort of Baranov, von Langsdorff said that it was extraordinary how often the reputation of a man is alone sufficient to strike panic into his antagonists and to accomplish the purpose he undertook without striking a stroke.

Among Baranov's creative schemes for wringing pelts from land, water, or other hunters and traders, was his decision to encroach and to poach on English and Spanish coastal waters to the south. He had to suspend this plot, being almost continually without transportation. But he was patient, and had only to wait like the trapdoor spider, and the sea would eventually carry to his lair almost anyone or anything he desired.

In 1803, at the lowest ebb of his fortunes, a Yankee skipper, Joseph O'Cain, sailed to the doorstep with a proposition. Doubtless Baranov's shrewdness and business vision prompted him to gamble with the stranger in a joint venture to invade those southern waters. The undertaking proved profitable. In addition, it led to the fur company's establishing a foothold nine years later in norther Alta California. This was Ft. Ross, which served the company as a farm to provision their northern settlements, and as a hunting station, for the succeeding twenty-nine years — or until the hunting became too scanty to warrant the expense involved. A hunting station in the Farallon Islands off of San Francisco and another one at nearby Bodega Bay followed Ft. Ross.

In 1804, with only a handful of employees and 800 Aleuts, Baranov complied with orders from headquarters to establish a position from which to recapture Sitka and reestablish it. Then, with the rebirth behind him and the winter of 1805 upon him, the little dictator watched hunger and its mate, the scurvy, run rampant among his hunters.

The only plus for Baranov must have been the stockholder's continuing to rake in a greater income than the company proper, thanks to him. But, otters were growing so scarce that Baranov had to trade seal peltry when J. J. Astor's ship approached him for otter and with plans for the first of a long series of future trades. The diminishing fur resource saw scruples once held, jettisoned in favor of the international dog-eat-dog rivalry. Yankee captains began to adopt the law of the jungle, and with the waxing of competition and the waning of furs, included murder in their repertory of schemes for securing the prized pelts.

Baranov's fierce competition (individual hunters, and other compatriot fur companies with their own Proms) was often aggravated by their providing the natives liquor and guns. As a result, Baranov had to devise increasingly more and tougher means of retaliation against his rivals as well as new or improved capers for harvesting his share of the declining supply of pelts.

Ultimately, Baranov's driving his men to drive the natives, plus the company's neglect in sending food and necessaries caused even his men to attempt a revolt. It failed. By now Baranov ruled from his cannon-bedecked fortress at Sitka and he was wearing a chainmail shirt. But this was only a portion of the manager's arsenal: he had other means of convincing besides brute force and rum: a talent for verbal persuasion, to boot.

In 1805 the Lewis and Clark Expedition to the mouth of the Columbia River disclosed the existence of the otter fur to President Jefferson and his people far to the east of the fur fields now well on their way to exhaustion.

By this year Baranov had founded Yakhutat (New Russia), also destined for massacre and burning. Fleeing this, one Prom and two hundred Aleuts perished at sea (the baidarka canoe is not infallible). Surely now Baranov, the invincible, faced a nut too hard to crack? Not at all, for at that juncture help blew into port not only singly, but twofold. First, his company's Baron Nikolai Rezanov arrived to inspect the station. Second, the Boston brigantine JUNO arrived with a cargo of tradegoods and provision — a godsend to the scurvy-ridden and famished Sitka colony.

Rezanov, on finding the distressed status of his company's settlement with sixty of the 192 residents dead or incapacitated, recognized it as a result of his company's negligence. As soon as the JUNO put in he purchased it, divided the cargo, and set sail for the little presidio of San Francisco in that golden land to the south for provision to nourish the Sitka employees.

Rezanov's voyage served another purpose. In fact, one strong school of thought sees his true mission as scouting for a site to establish a hunting station in these yet-to-be-exhausted fur fields. The years 1805 and 1806 presented an opportune time to gain a foothold, as Spain and France were distracted by Napoleon, and England was occupied with embryonic United States of America as well as with the little corporal.

Either Rezanov or his Alta California sweetheart, Concepcion Arguello, wheedled the Spanish authorites into bending their policy against trading with foreigners, and the baron obtained a cargo of grains, legumes, and other provision, to carry north. What Rezanov paid was $25,000 Spanish dollars (according to von Langsdorff), but JUNO's cargo of tradegoods offered the Californians the temptation to trade. They were similarly neglected by their government, seldom seeing their own provincial supply ships touching at their

PATIENT FREE-LOADER floats near California Otter hauled out on kelp-covered rock. (R.L. Branson Photo)

Alta California ports with necessities and a few luxuries such as those of the JUNO's cargo: ribbons, rum, flour, fishhooks, tools, cloth, household effects, clothing, mirrors, molasses.

By 1812, when Baranov established Ft. Ross, his stock in the north was principally fur seal peltry. Another woeful circumstance was appearing on his horizon: besides the growing scarcity of otters through shortsightedness and by dint of killing the goose, etc., the young generation of Aleuts and Alaskans had neither the skills nor the desire to hunt the mammal that their antecedents had. The traditional dependence on the otter must have been diluted by its scarcity as well as the adoption of fabric garments introduced by the European invader. Furthermore, now no longer a race, the natives were often as degenerate and as sickly as their oppressors. Imported diseases had eradicated entire villages. The survivors had not the stamina of their forebears for coping in so forbidding a climate as theirs, a land of storm and hell on earth. Time marched on, and their ambition was not what it had once been. Worse was the reduction in their numbers.

The only plus was that the decline in the skilled hunters permitted the remaining otters a reprieve. Perhaps the species would have been exterminated, like the passenger pigeon or the plains buffalo, had it not been for the decline of the expert hunter.

The Russian American Fur Company's last manager left in 1820, to be succeeded by governors. The Russians' last consignment of northern otter pelts to Siberia was a laboriously collected 8000. But their ship was wrecked, with the cargo swallowed up in Davey Jones' locker, and of value or service to no one.

It is likely that the combined hunting brotherhood ravished Alaska, its islands, the Aleutian chain, and Siberia's coast of fifty million dollars in otter pelts between 1745 and 1820. One means of calculating this uninflated figure was by that of the imperial tribute extracted from the Russian hunters. This amounted to a tithe (ten percent) paid on approximately three-fourths of a million pelts. Some historians believe that an equal number of pelts failed to reach the market, lost to shipwrecks principally, in the tempest-driven seas Bering and Pacific.

The Great Hunt's progress from the inhuman exploitation of fellow humans to unintentional genocide closely parallels the Spanish conquest of Central and South America. There the attraction was gold metal, whereas in the northeastern Pacific it was otter gold. As to relative wealth extracted, some reckon on the profit in otter furs to equal the value of all the gold taken throughout the sixteenth, seventeenth and eighteenth centuries from the Americas and shipped to Seville.

For twenty-nine years Ft. Ross remained a base of operations for the Russian American Fur Company hunters and as a farm to supply their counterparts in Alaska. The period also witnessed some ugliness, with the Aleuts being deposited on the islands off California where they made life miserable for the natives. The Russians took 50,000 of the 150,000 otters believed to live between Baja and Alaska.

By 1841, precisely a century after the Russians opened the fur rush in the northeastern Pacific, the otter population was so much reduced that the company sold Ft. Ross lock, stock, and barrel, to California's enterprising Captain John Sutter of Sacramento. With this the Russians retreated to their former haunts in the cold country. Before selling Seward's Folly to the United States in 1867 they hunted and traded such land furbearers as foxes, and followed such enterprises as purveying ice to our argonauts in California's Mother Lode.

After the Russians abandoned Alta California and their Ft. Ross, other hunters took batches of five thousand otters from the coast between Alaska and Baja California over the following twenty years. The species reached the edge of extinction by the end of the century, and with no lesson learned from the overharvesting of the northern otter colonies, which had driven the Russians to seek out the southern branch in the first place.

FIFTEEN
Spain And England In The North

SPAIN, of all nations, had one of the most advantageous positions for participation in the otter commerce. Why did she not press her advantage? She even traded with the Orient between mid-1500 and 1800 via the Manila Galleon plying between Mexico, or New Spain, and the Philippine Islands. Indirectly she traded with China by this same means.

As early as 1733 a Spaniard of New Spain discovered the otter off of Baja California. Perhaps one reason that this find was ignored was that Spain and her colonies had no need for fur garments to fend off cold weather. As food, otter would have meant nothing to them. Also, the Galleon was forbidden trade with Baja or with Alta California residents or merchants. So, when Californians began to hunt the otter, the Galleon dared not deal with them because of this prohibition — even when these trading ships at last became aware of the China fur market possibilities.

No one knew the northern boundary of Spain's Pacific coast north of Baja California, until she settled in Alta California in 1769 in an effort to occupy it. By so doing she gave warning to England and to Russia (and possibly to France) as well as to freebooters and expeditions labeled *scientific* or *discovery* that roamed the seven seas.

In 1774 Spain again got nervous and sent an expedition by sea as far north as southern Alaska. Enroute the crew discovered that the natives were enchanted by the abalone shells that the sailors had collected on beaches to the south. In trade they received furs, among them the otter's.

The following year Spain repeated the voyage but in addition planted a cross near today's Sitka, declaring the territory Spain's. It is likely that the Russians knew of this ceremonial act of possession, but Spains's colonies were spread so far and wide that every sovereign nation knew that she could not patrol all of them. She could not even do so along Baja and Alta California, so how could she monitor the far north, another thousand or so miles from her northernmost presidio, San Francisco?

The crews of this expedition anticipated trade and brought tradegoods to give in exchange for furs: the usual metal items, beads, clothing.

At this point one of Captain Cook's voyages of discovery revealed to him the seal and the otter and their abundance off of Vancouver Island. The find was broadcast to the world by the international grapevine and by the books published about the voyages. This motivated Spain to join the otter fur-trading circles, but it would be a few years before she got underway in its commerce proper.

By the mid-1770s it became apparent that her interest in the far north was dwindling, and limited now to the rich Nootka vicinity (Vancouver Island), instead of to the frigid zones to its north. She clung stubbornly to this locale to which she had withdrawn, as we shall see.

By 1785 Spain was ready and willing to let one of her businessmen convince her that she should participate in the windfalls that the fur trade had bestowed on some individuals of other nations. One Basadre y Vega pointed out that New Spain's silver mining industry demanded quicksilver and that China had this element in abundance. Trading with furs seemed just the ticket, and Basadre y Vega received the commission as sole trader for Spain.

He launched his monopoly with the following ground rules: the missionaries were to serve as agents for the pelts their neophytes harvested. The governor drew up a proclamation adding to the ground rules: the natives outside of the Missions were forbidden to sell a pelt to a soldier or to a settler, but were to sell to either a mayor or a commander of a presidio. Anyone selling to soldiers or to citizens of California would be punished.

Payment was between a real (twelve and one-half cents, or a bit) and a peso, except in the case of neophyte-to-padre. Presumably the padres paid in kind, not cash.

Although Basadre y Vega's enterprises fizzled by 1790 after but five years of life, pelts harvested and handled amounted to $87,000 in the Philippines. The embryonic project failed for numerous reasons: furs were not as numerous as anticipated, the Indians were neither motivated, forced, nor as skilled as their northern counterparts, the quality of the furs was not equal to that of the northern furs, Spain lacked experience in preparing furs and selling them, and there were diplomatic obstacles in China to affect the trading. And so on...

In 1788 Spain attempted to eject the British nationals established and hunting at Nootka, that furclad bay on the west coast of Vancouver Island. In relation to the johnny-come-lately Spaniards, England had squatter's rights here. Nevertheless, by 1789 Spain managed to establish a post there and maintained it until 1794. Apparently this maneuver was to prove her prior rights, and was not meant for hunting headquarters.

But it was too late in time for this. From Spain's settling here came an onsite clash to go down in history as the 1788 Nootka Affair, which at long last cleared up the nebulous proprietorship of that corner of the New World. The dispute resulted directly from the seizure of some English vessels by a pair of ships from New Spain: these ships, the Spanish charged, were trespassing. And this incensed the English sufficiently to threaten war with Spain despite their preoccupation with the colonies on the Atlantic coast.

Although obviously she was aggressive enough for a change, Spain had bark but not bite. She was eligible for support from her ally, France, but had to forfeit it: France was in the throes of her revolution. Spain retreated, unable to confront the English navy alone.

The treaty issuing from the Nootka dispute generously allowed England not only the rights to trade, but the privilege of settling anywhere to the north of San Francisco. Here is what Spain gained: England was prohibited trade with any of Alta California's citizens, a restriction made undoubtedly in reference to trade in furs.

Although the treaty terminated Spain's exclusive rights to the territory north of San Francisco, it did not terminate her well-ingrained error: failing to expend in order to expand. While no nation could have been raking in pelf by dint of robbery at such a rate as she had been doing since the early 1500s in the New World, Spain refused to spend what was essential to explore and to colonize the north coast. She pulled in her horns and helplessly watched the enterprise of her European neighbors take its course.

It was in 1788 also that the Siberian merchant, Grigori Shelikov, arrived in the vicinities of what we know as Sitka and Kodiak. He came to set the fur hunting and trading on its way toward an organized business, with the founding of his Russian American Fur Company. Shelikov was responsible for the brilliant choice of company manager, Aleksandr Baranov, which act freed himself to concentrate on securing the imperial monopoly from the Tsarina.

Shelikov planted a series of wooden posts (not crosses) to indicate possession of Sitka, with the intention of claiming the region for his own fatherland.

McCracken[5] and others believe that had it not been for Enhydra'a attracting Russia, leading to her holdings in the northeastern Pacific, England surely would have claimed the region along with her claim on Canada. And that means the United States would not have been likely to acquire Alaska and the Aleutians.

If Spain had colonized at the mouth of the Columbia River or at Bodega Bay in northern Alta California, almost certainly she would have scotched the Russian attempt to settle there with Ft. Ross in 1812.

Spain did consider making these occupations, but feared additional conflicts and their consequent cost in gold. Thus she dropped the role of dog in the manger only to a degree, continuing to hold unwittingly all of that real estate of the coast including golden California for those thirteen colonies far to the east.

SIXTEEN

Spain And Mexico In California

BY 1790 Spain's brief dip into the otter fur trade was finished, the commerce returned to the private sector and to the missionaries. Soon the gringo smugglers would provide the padres a finer market than the Basadre y Vega market, although trade with the foreigner continued forbidden. There were many ways to circumvent the law, however.

The spartan Alta California settlers and the Missions wanted and needed tools, furnishings, fabrics, molasses, rum and many other tradegoods from the cargos of the foreign ships. By hook or by crook, trading was bound to take place.

The early 1800s saw the Alta California Mission's most flourishing days. They also saw Ft. Ross established north of San Francisco by the Russians. In fact, governor Arguello contracted with its Russian American Fur Company to hunt on shares. The Russians supplied the Aleut hunters, while the governor contributed food and ten Indians to watch the Aleuts (whatever that meant).

Fr. Luis Martinez, one of the padres who made and kept his Missions economically healthy, brought looms to his neophytes. On these he taught them to weave woollens for trade as well as for clothing themselves. Another of his brainchildren was the training of his Indians to hunt the otter.

Fr. Jose Sanches, another priest, was even more assertive in the fur trade. His activities seem to exemplify the Spanish sea otter quest along Alta California's central coast. According to a journal

left by one of the many Yankee fur trappers coming overland in the
early 1800s:

> Fr. Sanches had a brig commanded by Captain William
> Richardson, an Englishman , which was engaged in the trade
> between California and other parts of Mexico and Peru, to
> transport him and his shooting party to some point on the coast
> where the otter resorted. Fr. Sanches intrusted Captain Rich-
> ardson to lend such aid and assistance as were at his disposal
> to fit out the party. The brig was lying in the port of San Pedro
> to which place the party repaired about the first of July. With
> the help of the ship-carpenter of the brig two canoes were made.
> Timbers for the canoe were cut on the Feliz rancho near Los
> Angeles, and the planks made from inch pine boards brought
> from Boston in a Boston vessel trading on the coast. The boards
> after being sawed into strips about five inches in width were
> split into long boards of less than half an inch in thickness. This
> cutting and splitting was done with a hand saw.
>
> Early in July the canoes and some stores were taken on board
> the brig and Mr. Young with his otter hunters numbering six
> besides himself of whom two were Kanakas and myself, em-
> barked and the brig stood out seaward. Calling at the Island
> of Santa Cruz the brig anchored at Prisoners' harbor where the
> water casks were filled for the ship's use and then sailing to Pt.
> Conception the otter hunters, their canoes and some stores of
> which no part was whisky, were landed. The brig's yawl was
> also left with the hunters. The brig then proceeded on her voy-
> age to Monterey and the bay of San Francisco. After a few days
> spent in otter shooting near Pt. Conception Mr. Young, who
> had been spilled out of a canoe into the surf a number of times,
> left the otter hunters to continue the shooting and the past-
> time of being spilled out of canoes into the laughing surf, and
> proceeded to Monterey by land.[7]

Later, with what the trapper described as the moral and material
aid of Fr. Sanches, the party cut timber and sawed plank in the
mountains, carried these to San Pedro on oxcarts. There the wood
was converted into a 30-ton schooner, and it made sail for Baja's
otter colonies where it spent an entire year, returning to hunt as far
north as Pt. Conception.

SEATTLE AQUARIUM family of three females, one male (1978), includes this clam-eater. (Doug Wilson Photo for Seattle Aquarium)

Fr. Sanches collaborated thoroughly in otter hunting, but perhaps only with foreign trappers who by some means secured a license from Mexico for the purpose. There were several routes to this: one could marry a Mexican citizen and obtain a license in his or (usually) her name; one could become a Mexican citizen through naturalization; one could work with a partner who was a citizen and thus eligible for license. Captain William Dana, a famous Yankee who married into a landed grandee family and in addition granted 35,000 acres of his own, was for a time the port captain of Santa Barbara. He had a license which he distributed (for one percent of the haul) to whichever foreigner he chose to do business with.

In the early 1840s John Wilson (later Juan) joined a partner and got a loan for the purpose of making an otter expedition both in Baja and Alta California. Results were fine, but Wilson lost many of his hunters before the journey ended: they claimed their boss was too stingy to feed them well, and they left, hungry.

Wilson also became a grantee of thousands of acres of Alta California land, and married an Alta Californian who owned other great acreages formerly granted to her family.

SEVENTEEN

The Yankees

FRANCE and Portugal were represented in the fur rush, but on a smaller scale than England, Russia and the budding nation on the Atlantic coast.

The Yankees were a bit tardy but appeared onstage thanks to John Ledyard, a seaman with Captain Cook. Arriving home, he tipped off the capitalists among his compatriots, thereby changing many a tack for those world-ranging trading ships, the Boston Clippers. From 1800 forth they would trade furs the entire length of the furlined Pacific coast from San Diego to the arctic. The furs they traded for with their cargo from New England they then traded in the Orient for those coveted porcelains, silks, spices, that their compatriots fancied.

Gradually the Boston captains gained the advantage over both Russian and English competitors in the trade from Vancouver northward. Both Russian and English traders were hampered in getting furs to the Chinese: England gave her east India Company the monopoly of trade with China, and the Russians were limited to trading through one inland trade center: the border of Mongolia. Other nationals could sail into any port to trade, whatever their cargo.

In 1788 the United States naval Captains Gray and Kendricks dipped into the Hunt in the fruitful Vancouver Island vicinity. Gray's first transaction was the exchange of an old chisel for the equivalent at that time of $8000 worth of furs!

The Boston captains and the English were represented as the shrewdest traders in the field. By carrying the best quality and the greatest abundance of tradegoods they outdistanced the Russians in the competition. Some historians claim that the Yankee traders approached the villages "trading, cajoling, conniving, intimidating, and conducting themselves like demons possessed."

The Russians, in order to wrest more pelts, and faster, fell back on more force: the turning of the screw, as it were. Their methods of extraction included approaching the natives in an armed boat as they were hunting, and confiscating their collection of furs. If any objection arose, the Russian practice was to silence it with muskets.

Even small-scale civil war among the Russian compatriots was possible in this period of desperation to secure the remaining pelts. Such was the competition to ship furs to a common fatherland that if one of the Russian hunting parties clashed with another one over possession of a band of native hunters, the rule was to battle for the privilege of exploiting it. The alternative to this gambit was the combining of the competing gangs for joint-exploitation of the unfortunate prize, the hunters.

Yankee hunters and traders continued ferreting out the lonely residual otters among the bights, nooks, and crannies in which they had secreted themselves like a handful of the California Indians after the Yankee occupation. Hunter schooners carried on them another remnant: Aleut hunters, by now carrying muskets with the magic bullet (which perhaps compensated for their fading ambition and expertise).

The last stand of the otter was in the Aleutian Sanak Islands, whose climate had the reputation of a maritime inferno. Perhaps the white hunters and traders reserved until the bitter-end hunting in such a hellish climate.

SECTION FOUR
FRIENDS AND ENEMIES

EIGHTEEN

The Art Of Hunting The Otter, CNGATUQ

WHEN a native of the Aleutian Islands wriggled into his snug, cork-light baidarka (canoe or kayak) to go otter-hunting, he checked his amulet before reaching for his double paddle. The charm was either of stone or of bone, and fashioned in the likeness of his quarry. Its purpose: to reduce the otter's cunning. The Aleuts believed that the otter had human origins, little wonder in light of the creative inventions Enhydra produced in an effort to elude his predator, man.

An Aleutian folktale describes the source of the sea otter as a young couple of Aleuts who were not allowed to marry under one of their cultural tabus. They solved their dilemma by leaping into the sea from an island cliff. Immediately they were transformed into otters, and as their anguished families and friends watched one swam to the east and the other to the west, and out of view.

By the time European man arrived among them the 30,000 Aleutians had accumulated a storehouse of knowledge of the anatomy of the mammals in the waters around their islands. The Aleuts may have arrived in the western hemisphere some eight thousand years ago, but by two thousand years ago they had learned to capture the sea animals, becoming dependent upon them for food, clothing, shelter; even for transportation. Their seagoing thistledown kayaks were of sea lion hide. These were portable by one hand, some twenty feet long, and only two feet through the beam. Their slender frame was of driftwood, since little timber grew in the rocks and tundra of the islands.

Those hunters among the Aleuts who were the most skillful and courageous were almost worshipped, but it was not bringing home the otter that earned these men the highest honors from their community. It was the whale. This was the creature demanding the greatest art and courage from the man who would capture it. However, an English captain in the late 1700s wrote, 'Compared to taking the whale, the taking of the sea otter is attended with far greater hazard as well as trouble, with bow, arrow, small harpoon, several fathoms of line for dragging the otter to the boat... Bringing the otter to boat a fierce battle ensues, with hunters frequently wounded by claws and teeth.'

In the opinion of author Harold McCracken[5], who wrote so colorfully and authentically of the hunt in the northeastern Pacific Ocean, the otter gave his pursuers a chase both difficult and dangerous, for such a meek animal. Reason: the invention and cunning of Enhydra.

When the Siberians arrived, they found the Aleut race hunting otter by means of the spearing surround, eventually to use the musket, and later the rifle. Multiple baidarkas would hunt together and on sighting an otter would attempt to close in around it like a drawstring. The otter would sound, remain below as long as possible, and when he surfaced at last for oxygen, the hunter closest to him would try to spear or harpoon it. If the otter escaped, the procedure would continue until repeated dives and too little time to remain at the surface to draw breath exhausted the animal. Prevented from grooming in this situation, the pelage would become saturated, and either slow down his progress or pull down the otter, drowning him.

In the forced marches of the Russians native fleets of two-man baidarkas, one man would paddle with the other serving as observer and hunter. When the victim was hauled in, the hunter would lean over the side to skin it, then stow the pelt at his feet.

So numerous and efficient were the hunters that they terrorized their prey to the point of developing in the younger generations something akin to race memory. The pups themselves showed their fear of humans, and apparently without signal from their sophisticated elders, the juveniles shot off in the opposite direction from any scent of humankind drifting to them in the breezes.

The hunters were so relentless that the mammals not only began to spend more time at sea, but produced methods of escape which impressed their predators with their ingenuity. Reports such as that about the otter's withdrawing an arrow with his teeth sound highly exaggerated; nonetheless they exist. Despite his sharp wits, the otter was handicapped: he possessed neither speed nor a refuge in which to hide from the hunter. For hiding he had only kelp and rocks. One trick he used to postpone death in the serious game of hide-and-seek, was to slip under the baidarka beyond reach of the hunter and his weapon.

Another was to head shoreward toward the rip current. This piling-up of the incoming waves near the shore could upset the Aleut's almost unupsettable craft. Hiding in a sea cave was another escape gambit: while the tide was ebbing this crevice in a reef was open, allowing the otter air to breathe. If a net was tossed over the mouth of the cave until the incoming tide filled the crevice, the otter drowned.

Enhydra'a adversary learned a few tricks besides this one. Naturalist Georg Steller, who accompanied Bering, wrote that the otters' love for their young is so intense that for them they expose themselves to the most manifest danger of death. Taking advantage of a mother otter's love and instinct, the men would capture a pup to bait her. By squeezing the pup until it whimpered or wailed, the mother would be compelled to approach the babe. Also, leaving a pup on a beach or on a snarl of kelp at sea surrounded by stout fishhooks often trapped adults. An occasional tug on the line was enough to snag the otter answering the pup's cries of distress.

Reports from the 150-year long Great Hunt showed Enhydra capable of committing suicide under the enemy's relentless pursuit: rather than surrender he might choose to wedge himself between underwater rocks to drown himself.

On and from the shore hunters found it easy to harvest otters. Approaching them as they rested on the shore during a noisy storm or high winds, the hunters clubbed them with a pole, even stabbed them — for the mammals moved slowly and sluggishly when earthbound. Snow[3], writing of his hunting days in the Kuriles, said that he and his men would go out early in the morning to catch the beached otters. They reasoned that the cold forced them to haul out. (His own beard, Snow said, would freeze together and he had to crack the ice with his fingers.) Sometimes these meek little animals would resist with teeth and claw, he said, so that the hunters' boots would suffer accordingly.

Late in the hunt derricks of timber were built on the shore with a rifleman stationed on it. The rifle made it a cinch to kill otter in the sea, then the wind or tide carried the body near the foot of the tower.

Mexicans and Yankees hunted in the south with rifles by canoe or by rowboat. The rifleman stood in the boat relying on his crew to respond quickly to his orders, carrying him to within bullet's range of his prey. Since there were often a number of boats hunting together, the risk of being shot in the crossfire was great. "There is no danger in a bullet you can hear" was the byword for that style of hunting.

Snow told of a legendary Mexican rifleman who on one hunt shot seventeen otters while standing on a pair of two-inch planks, his men paddling about recovering the otters as fast as he shot them.

Snow's choice of weather conditions most conducive for such a hunt was a smooth sea, and what he called a "lifted" fog: one hovering fifty or more feet above the water. This gave both a milky appearance to the surface and visibility of considerable distance to a dark object.

Kelp canopies helped the hunters; they smoothed the surface seas like oil. Snow claimed that the heaviest of seas could not break in a kelp bed.

NINETEEN

Friends And Enemies

THAT Enhydra has been evolving toward the marine milieu in the fashion of other terrestrial species for eons is true. However, did he not accelerate the process during the Great Hunt? Not the process of physically adapting to the sea, but merely moving into it totally even though his body and some of his habits were terrestrial in nature. Of course this applies more to the southerner, nereis, than to the northerner, lutris.

Following the hunt's initial and immense depredations among the northern otter population, reports described some lutris colonies moving farther out to sea, returning closer to shore or to shore proper less frequently. But the southerner said farewell in toto, with only an occasional visit of a solitary otter to the strands. Obviously the pacific disposition of the Pacific Ocean from Canada south permitted him to be born and bred in its waters. The frequency of storms in the less benign north Pacific and in the Bering Sea forced the northerner periodically to seek cubbies and havens among the rocks, hills and dales of island terrain.

The southern otter population's decision to desert land totally seems almost a trade-off with nature: in exchange for escaping man's harassment nereis accepted the unceasing, round the clock task of (one)keeping warm (or cool) and keeping the skin dry, and (two) foraging to nourish his still-out-of-its element body. Since he was to remain in the sea, he would need more calories than when he divided his time between land and sea.

But, in this trade nature provided ample and easily harvested nourishment. Apparently, too, in the exchange the otter gained the time for this pair of demanding chores only because he gained a home with few natural enemies to hide or run from. The literature does not give much information on natural or marine predators until the otter studies under the federal government began after World War II. Since then the white shark (*Cacharodon carcharias*) has been blamed for killing southern otters, but evidence has been more circumstantial than material: a tooth left in each of a pair of otter carcasses. However, with the increase in the otter population this has changed. In 1977 a California biologist counted four otters killed by sharks: two in the northern region of the range and two in the southern. He has evidence of eleven attacks by sharks in the last score of years, and now suspects that ninety deaths formerly attributed to boat propellers may have been caused by sharks.

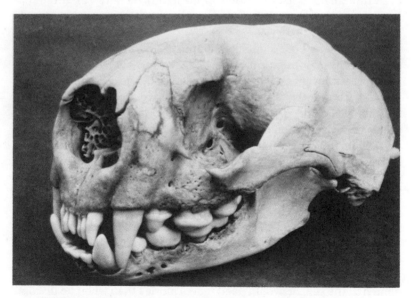

WHITE SHARK predation is documented by shark's tooth embedded in the base of this otter skull. (DFG Photo)

The killer whale (*Orcinus orca*) on whose feeding path all otters live, relishes the sea lion, elephant seal and fur seal. He is expected to fancy the otter but concrete evidence of this is lacking. Many people have reported seeing him spook Enhydra, but have not seen him eating Enhydra.

A biologist in the Russian Commander Islands caught sight of a herd of whales heading toward shore, and a terrified pod of otters bolting to the rocky points and beaches to scramble out of reach. And yet, other reports from the north show that the otters singly do not become agitated when a killer whale cruises close by. Either they rise high in the water to get a better view of the whale, they slowly move away, or they move into the shelter of the kelp canopy.

In 1958 a biologist witnessed an astonishing sight off southern California: a trick that Orcas used for earning a dinner. A bull whale charged a large inshore rock on which a group of sea lions was sunning. Although the impact against the rock stunned the whale, in a moment he was feeding on the pinnipeds that had leaped into the sea and into the jaws of death!

In the north the bald eagle had been considered an enemy to the sea otter because otter remains had been found in the nests. Also, someone reported having seen an eagle carry off a live pup. But as a rule pups floated alone on the sea while eagles went about their business. Like everything else, this changed, too: off of Amchitka the increase in the eagle population has increased the incidence of otter-predation since 1968. In preparing for Cannikin, the explosion of a nuclear device under Amchitka, the many humans involved accumulated a refuse dump. Apparently this helped to feed the eagle population, almost doubling it between 1968 and 1972. A 1976 report in *Pacific Discovery* magazine claimed that the otter pups, helpless for their first month, comprised a good share of the eagle's diet. Of the thirty percent of the daily diet which is mammals, three-quarters of it is otter pup. As many as nine pups were taken to a single nest during a four-week period, and in twenty-eight of thirty-four nests examined, otter pup remains were found.

Observers report both eagles and gulls swooping around feeding otters and snatching meat from them. Gulls are particularly troublesome for the dining otter; they are bold and have stick-to-itiveness beyond measure, floating alongside the otter waiting to snatch a

GULLS harass otters for morsels of shellfish, an easy way to get a meal. (Franklin Enos Photo)

morsel of his food. Sometimes the otter will splash water at the pests with his flipper, or will dive repeatedly. But all is in vain.

Among the myriad questions remains this one: why did the Russians' captive otters have such fear of some of the birds flying through their cage? If they were freeloaders like the gulls, were they not more of a nuisance than a menace?

At the end of the 1960s, of eleven southern otter carcasses washed ashore, official examination revealed the causes to be gunshot wounds, heavy blows, and deep cuts. In 1970, of twenty-five postmortem examinations, eighteen were determined as unnatural. Six were probably victims of boating accidents, three drowned accidentally in capture attempts by authorities, three in captivity, four had been shot and two died of bacterial infections attributed to improperly treated sewage.

During the first ten and one-half months of 1977 eighty-four carcasses were found in the southern range. Four of these were believed caused by shootings, one in the north and three in the south. The previous year, 1976, ninety were found. For the years 1973, 1974, 1975, and 1976, the body counts were 84, 45, 52, and 67.

In the mid-1970s the southern sea otter authority, Judson Vandevere, reported that the two most common causes of death resulted from boat impact and gunshot. Since 1964, he said, 168 necropsy findings indicated that although the cause of death was not determined in 55 cases, 47 appeared to have died from propeller lacerations or boat impact, and 19 were shot.

TWENTY

Other Otter Friends And Enemies

ALTHOUGH external parasites are not known to plague Enhydra, it appears that the southern branch is infested with an intestinal worm. Biologists found in the early 1970s that 86% of the carcasses carried it.

Susie, the contented female living in Seattle's Woodland Zoo between 1955 and 1961, lived in freshwater. (She was from the Aleutians.) The necropsy after her death indicated only an infestation of mites in the nasal passages. Perhaps a pool of seawater would have prevented the tragic development; that is, if the parasites were indeed the cause of her death.

The lutris is infested by a variety of internal parasites, but these rarely appear the cause of death. External parasites seem to be unusual.

Surely the most baffling cause of death in a sea otter was discovered in 1976. An adult southern male that beached itself at Morro Bay (the southern portion of the range) was flown to Sea World where he lived for a fortnight, then died.

Among his symptons was below-normal coordination. His death was due to *coccidioidomycosis*, or San Joaquin Valley fever. Inland, beyond the coast range, lies the vast San Joaquin, locale of the dissease and source of the particular fungus responsible for it.

Dr. Kenyon[4] divides causes of sea otter mortalities into two groups when they occur during the late winter or early spring in the north. One group consists of those whose death was caused by injury or disease; the other consists of those which show evidence of starvation and exhibit symptoms of enteritis.

Stress, he says, may activate in the otter the organism *clostridium*, present in all animals. This leads to enteritis, often the terminal symptom of death in the otter of Amchitka Island, home of the largest lutris colony. Environmental stress can produce chilling; it also can be responsible for an otter's failure to get enough nourishment. In winter and early spring, when the habitat may not be able to carry the entire colony it is hard for any age of otter to forage during a storm.

The weak, old, or very young are unable to catch the fish and the octopus that the healthy adults can, and must fall back on the benthic organisms such urchins or shellfish, much reduced in quantity and in size at that time.

They are also more easily cast against the rocks and injured or killed. The healthy adults are likely to carry a bit of stored fat, too; the others are not.

Dr. Kenyon noted that healthy adults spend less time on shore (as indicated by animals captured there) during periods of storm than do emaciated juveniles and old adults. Also, seventy-five percent of the annual Alaskan mortality coincides with periods of maximum wind velocity in the late winter/early spring seasons. Most dead otters are found on or near favored hauling out or resting areas where they crawl out to die.

In California, also, the number of sea otter carcasses and live animals recovered can be directly related to storms and sea surface turbulence. Here are excerpts from a paper by veterinarians of Sea World, San Diego:

> A review of the literature indicates that most field researchers generally agree upon the conditions and causes relative to sea otter mortalities... The numbers of dead and moribund animals found on the beaches usually increases after periods when environmental stresses are the greatest. The data indicate that the stormy periods of late winter and early spring take the highest toll on the sea otter.[8]

When food is scarce at home, why don't otters in the islands migrate to less-populated ones? If the distance is short enough to cross without having to feed, then the depth of the passage between islands is not a factor. But to navigate a long passage, the otter must feed, and if the depth is greater than thirty fathoms (180 feet) the chances are that he cannot succeed in reaching the bottom to forage.

One of the principal purposes of the otter's interest in kelp is that the canopies of this seaweed are havens of calm in a rough sea. Kelp acts like oil poured on troubled waters.

The smoothing effect of offshore kelp beds has always been sought by small coasting vessels seeking their protection whenever possible in order to land their cargo.

This seaweed (both *Macrocystis* and *Nereocystis*) is indeed the otter's best friend. It is a supermarket providing homes for stars, fish, snails, and sundry other food organisms preferred by Enhydra. Often it is snarled enough to sustain a pup while its mother goes browsing. The otters lie in or near it for a nap, secure that they are not likely to drift shoreward under these circumstances, with a stipe of the alga draped over their belly to anchor themselves. Or the mothers moor their pups in this manner, assured that the pup will be there when they return.

Kelp and the otter are meant for each other. The latter finds protective coloring — even texture — among its branches. The bladders on one variety are spherical and almost as large as an otter's wet head. The otter keeps down the urchin population which is a kelp-grazer. Lastly, kelp is important to man; it is a major industry providing one of the ingredients in many products from ice cream to paint to tooth paste.

One half million substances wash down our streams or are flushed through outfall pipes directly into the Pacific Ocean. Jacques Cousteau claims that man is killing his oceans; that the seas are more polluted than the land. As early as 1969 an otter found dying on a beach near Monterey had nose sores which had prevented his diving to forage. In the nostrils were bacteria found in human and in animal wastes.

The chemicals running to the seas include pesticides and industrial wastes (petroleum products, such as dry-cleaning solvents, crankcase oil). Some pesticides stop the spawning of shellfish; others spare adult organisms, but kill the young. As long as we dispose of wastes by the primitive method of dilution we must not be surprised that we poison the seas and the life in them.

In 1970 a study determined that food species of the southern otter *nereis* contain significant levels of cadmium, copper and zinc, after finding high levels of these in otter tissues. Two years later the cadmium level in the liver tissue had doubled.

Increasing concentrations of DDE and PCB in otter tissue, plus other organo-chlorine pesticides, were emerging in the mid-1970s. (Large concentrations of DDT and PCB are known to cause reproductive damage in sea lions.)

California offshore oil drilling is on the increase. The chances for spillage from oil tankers, either accidental or by purposeful flushing of bilges are increased with the tankers expanding in both numbers and girth. These ply the coast, the entire length of the otter habitat from the Aleutians to southern California. The Alaska Department of Fish and Game's primary concern at present is that oil and gas development will adversely affect their sea otter, Enhydra lutris lutris.

Near the southern border of the southerner's 230-mile range at least one tanker daily loads petroleum from a pipeline running into the sea. A ruptured line spilled crude oil there in the late 1960s. All the world has heard about the Santa Barbara oil disaster of the late 1960s, less than one hundred miles south of the California sea otter's present range.

Pleasure boat propellers (and presumably those of commercial fishing craft) have been growing into one of the major causes of death for the southerner. The other one, gunshots. Most of the boat accidents are reported in or near Monterey Bay, center of the otter population of California.

SECTION FIVE
RECENT HISTORY

TWENTY-ONE
North: Voices In The Wilderness

TOWARD the end of the dark pathway of the 150 years bent on the killing of the goose, etc., some perceptive individuals did see the handwriting and either warned against overharvesting or acted on preserving the otter species. They saw the parallel between the disappearance of the otter and that of the fur seal.

More importantly, after the United States bought Alaska one of our ministers alerted the Department of the Interior on the disastrous effects of Yankee enterprise on the welfare of the native human population. By 1895, otter in the north was commercially extinct, with only remnant populations scattered here and there. The hunting was narrowed down to the Aleutians where it all began, with Yanks carrying Aleut hunters (such as they were by that time) and their canoes with them by schooner. Now rifles made the scraping of the bottom of the barrel necessary, and the last barrel was the cluster of Sanak Islands.

Apparently our national approach was not to conserve until some time after we purchased Seward's Folly. A commander of our Bering Patrol fleet wrote in 1897 that the otter was being harassed: clubbed, shot on shore, caught in nets, their hauling grounds made almost uninhabitable by campfires of hunters and defiled by the fisheries and decaying bodies of their slaughtered companions.

Actually the officer's concern was for the Aleuts. He said that they were deprived of the chief means of their existence by the overkill of seal, sea lion, walrus, whale. Their salmon grounds were being invaded oversuccessfully by means of zealous fishing as well as the establishment of a commerce with its insatiable appetite.

When the population of the otter from Amchitka, along the west coast of Alaska, Canada, the United States and Baja California came close to extinction from overkill, the governments of Japan, Russia, Great Britain, and the United States drew up an agreement. It was aimed at conserving the fur seal, but someone with influence saw that the otter was included. The objective was the recovery of the fur resource utilized by the economy like other ventures in resources: oil, copper, ore, coal, natural gas, fish and shellfish.

By the time the international treaty among these sealing nations was drawn in 1911 fewer than two thousand otters remained. Most of them were off the more remote islands of the north, probably the reason they remained in the land o' living. Two thousand miles lay between these and the embryonic pod or colony of southern cousins off the central California coast.

On the eve of the signing of the treaty twenty-eight men in fourteen boats brought in a dozen otter pelts, which sold for $800 each. After that poaching and a black market continued: on one occasion seven furs brought $3500 — plus a $5000 fine.

In 1935, Coast Guardsmen stationed on the island of Amchitka were surprised to find sea otters off- and onshore. In 1936 the United States Biological Survey (now Bureau of Fisheries) sent an expedition to investigate. It also stationed agents on the islet to discourage poaching, since the picture of the otter continued to bring to most minds the picture of wealth. Since the international treaty's inception occasional instances of poaching and selling northern furs took place. Occasionally those involved found that the fines imposed on them as a result far exceeded the profits from their sales.

By 1939 the official census of the northern otter colony was 1700.

Few of us knew at that time what a sea otter was, and during World War II our G.I.'s were surprised and pleased to find "those goofy little animals playing offshore" to amuse them on their off-duty hours. The Enhydra population grew apace and in 1945 was believed to stand at about three thousand. In 1947 the Bureau of Fisheries again sent biologists to examine the status of the otter. At this point Dr.

Kenyon commenced his study, which resulted in the most comprehensive volume of information on the mammal that existed, doubtless, in the world.[4]

By 1949 officials began to find winter die-offs decimating the pods; the waters off of Amchitka could not sustain year around the burgeoning population of that furbearer.

With the continuing good health of the national economy in view, the government decided to transplant some otters to less crowded islands, reestablishing pods in historic habitats. The first experiment to capture and to relocate proved a failure, but was the impetus to invest in a research program to learn why the capture, holding, transporting of the peaceful creatures stymied the biologists and others involved.

REDISCOVERY of the California otter, 15 miles south of Carmel in 1938. No reliable report of a pod had been made since 1916; those who knew of these had kept the secret. (Laidlow Williams Photo)

As the 1950s dawned the census in the north was between six thousand and eight thousand otters. By 1954 it was obvious that more study was necessary and the USFWS began a second study of Enhydra whose handling defied the usual management procedures. It is probable that no one would have predicted the necessity to give some fifteen years to the research. But neither did anyone know the complexities of the physique and the psyche or temperament of Enhydra lutris lutris. However, by now the government believed otters plentiful enough that they could be harvested on a small scale from some of the more highly populated (otterwise) Aleutian islets.

The year 1959 brought Alaska into the Union as a sovereign state giving it jurisdiction over the otters within three miles of its shores, removing them from Uncle Sam's jurisdiction. This split the otter stewardship, giving the federal government control over the animals when on shore of the Amchitka Wildlife Refuge as well as when it swam or dwelled beyond territorial boundaries. By this time the entire Aleutian chain had been designated as a national wildlife refuge.

Thus Alaska was eligible to elect to harvest some furs, which it did in 1962 and again in 1963. Otter culling was a project of the Alaska Department of Fish and Game, not a concession awarded to the business community. In 1967 Alaska harvested again, at Amchitka and Adak. By the first of 1968 one thousand pelts were ready for the auction block. The resulting services were threefold. One, some revenue for Alaska's public treasury, but not up to expectations. Two, ample specimens made available for Alaska's and the federal biologists for research so necessary for the objective of otter management. Three, a revived valuable natural resource.

According to Dr. Kenyon in 1969, "Wise conservation practices based on biological knowledge will assure not only that the sea otter will once again be an article of commerce, but also that this interesting member of our wildlife community will flourish as an esthetically and scientifically valuable part of our environmental heritage." [4]

By 1978 the population in the north was between 100,000 and 140,000 of the mammals.

TWENTY-TWO

North: Project Cannikin

THE purpose of a United States Wildlife Refuge designation is to make human activity off limits while creating a sanctuary for resident and migratory birds and animals. When humans are allowed access to a wilderness area they enter under the strictest of rules made solely for the protection of that refuge's biota.

President Taft bestowed this designation upon the Aleutian Island chain in 1913, and it was narrowed to the island of Amchitka in 1936. Except for the World War II years when it served as a military base, the islet's refuge status was administered by the Department of the Interior.

Apparently the conditions under which the wildlife refuge category was made in this instance included one stating that it should not "interfere with the use of the island for lighthouse, military or naval purposes".

In 1960 the Atomic Energy Commission chose the island of Amchitka for experimenting with thermonuclear devices of great magnitude, but the secret plan accidentally reached President Kennedy, who cancelled it. In 1965 the AEC chose to detonate an 80,000 ton device 2300 feet beneath the island. In 1969, another one, of lesser magnitude at 8000 feet, and this time the allies (Pentagon and AEC) professed that the plan was top secret, thus pulling the wool over the eyes of the so-called guardian of the wildlife refuge, the Department of the Interior.

This time the otters were guinea pigs sealed with 50mm cannon within steel tanks for purposes of testing their shock threshold, according to the AEC. No one has explained publicly why Enhydra was tapped for this ghoulish project.

Overwhelming opposition to the Cannikin test of 1971 continued up to the eleventh hour, then failed. The governments of Japan and Canada, plus 70,000 petitioners from the province of British Columbia objected. And, knowing the Aleutians to be unstable and quake-prone, Alaskans, their Senator Gravel and thirty-six other senators appealed to the Congress and to the president. Even most of the federal agencies which were asked to study the potential impact on Amchitka's environment opposed it!

One wonders who did want the experiment with the five megaton bomb besides the AEC and its partner. The AEC refused to give a reason for it under the old saw of national security and despite the great clamor, President Nixon authorized the pushing of the button at the last moment before the scheduled detonation.

After the blast the AEC admitted that a number of otters (of the 8000 that called Amchitka home) had been killed, perhaps by a storm preceding Cannikin! A fortnight later it announced the recovery of only eighteen otters, but did not bother to say that storms had cancelled the search for dead animals only three days following the blast. This was in November, a stormy period.

Alaska's Fish and Game unit estimated that from 300 to 800 otters were missing, while other biologists calculated that over 1000 otters were dead. The AEC served to confuse the news as to the actual effects of Cannikin: the loss of between 1100 and 3300 otters, some on land in the dreadful uplift action, some crushed beneath rock slides, and others from overpressure while diving.

That sea otters were injured and killed was not the sole harm done. Surprisingly, the aftermath that the biologists feared most was the extent to which human activity from those many humans involved in the experiment would deteriorate the island's ecosystem.

It is nothing new for the Pentagon to choose such areas to destroy for so-called national defense purposes: the navy bombarded part of the Hawaiian Islands National Wildlife Refuge with the explanation that the destruction was for purpose of national defense.

One wonders just what is the significance of the wildlife refuge designation, if not to keep man and his destructive activities at bay?

TWENTY-THREE

South: Rediscovery Of The Sea Otter

DURING the 1920s and early 1930s convicts from California's prisons pick-and-shoveled a road along the state's coast at a snail's pace between San Simeon (northern San Luis Obispo county) and up through Big Sur country to the Monterey Peninsula. Heavy equipment finally replaced hand-labor and in the summer of 1937 the road was opened, christened the Roosevelt Highway. (Now, California One or Cabrillo Highway.)

In the Twenties some of the California Department of Fish and Game staff knew that the otter dwelled off the heart of this wilderness of Big Sur with its towering yellow bluffs and scanty human inhabitants. But, with good reason their existence was kept a secret until the new highway made the country accessible by motor and by foot. In 1938 a few residents looked closely at a pod of what they believed were sea lions, but guessed they were otters, and confirmed their guess by asking a warden.

The news of the revival of what was believed an extinct species spread rapidly from esoteric circles to the public, and by 1950 fans were visiting Pacific Grove and the Pt. Lobos State Reserve for an easy glimpse of what the state was calling its "esthetic natural resource". Too, observation pullouts along the highway encouraged tourists to hunt otter visually for themselves as the colony increased in population. The signs also warned that firearms were illegal if carried along the otter refuge.

Big Sur spans over 150 miles of the rough, rugged shoreline and uplands of both the San Luis Obispo and Monterey coast. Its inland slopes, clad in the densest of chaparral, lead to the coast range, its peaks often spattered with winter's snow, and the total wilderness of its deep-cleft valleys make it forbidding to humankind. One glimpse of this and the cliffs and jumbled folded reefs fingering out into the crashing breakers ceaselessly pounding at their underpinnings makes it clear why this was the southern otter's last stand.

Even with access made available to auto travel, and the increase in both commercial and pleasure boats plying this segment of the continental shelf, Big Sur remained the safest, snuggest habitat for the colony.

It was more the accelerated increase in fisherpeople and shellfisherpeople following World War II which held the kiss of death for who-knows-how-many otters, scions of the rediscovered Enhydra lutris nereis colony. At first they were believed sea lions (legal game) and considered a threat in the fisheries. Later, some of the fishermen shot the otters for what they were: competition in the shellfish beds.

The most recent court case, and hopefully the final one convicting anyone of killing sea otters off of the southern coast, was in 1972. For three men it brought fines of one thousand dollars, plus a three-year probation period. Hitherto there had been less risk of apprehension, but the fleet of patrol boats had increased, more pleasure craft were sailing and fishing, and more citizens alert to protecting their environment. In this instance, more than one of the many families overlooking Estero Bay in San Luis Obispo county who had telescopes in their windows reported the shooting to the authorities.

In the meantime the otter population of Enhydra lutris nereis expanded: in 1967, 562; in 1968, 483; and in 1971,902. (By this time the otter outgrew its federally endowed status as a *rare and endangered species.*) The 1972 census recorded 1060; 1974, 1163; and 1976, 1800 (last official census).

The Department of Fish and Game calculates the southern otter population is now increasing one to two percent annually, whereas until 1976 the increase was five percent per annum. *The Otter Raft*[9] of Winter, 1978, reports that the Department estimates that the population in the established portion of the range (Monterey Bay to Morro Bay) has reached equilibrium density.

SECTION SIX
THE CONTINUING CONFLICT

TWENTY-FOUR

Should Colonies Be Confined Or Free?

TWO MAJOR DISAGREEMENTS exist between Enhydra's champions and his opponents. The principal one is whether or not to confine the otters to their current range of 180 miles, or to allow them their head. Should they roam unrestricted until they settle of their own free will, eventually drawing their boundary lines themselves?

The second question: should the responsibility for the overharvesting of the shellfish population along California's coast be borne by man or otter? Which is responsible for the diminution of invertebrates such as abalone, clam, sea urchin, along the shoreline segments where the otter has lived or has journeyed as a transient?

Here are the opinions of Dr. Betty S. Davis, Research Associate in Zoology, Museum of Vertebrate Zoology, the University of California, Berkeley, as excerpted from her article in *Pacific Discovery* magazine (San Francisco Academy of Sciences, March/April 1977):

> After protection for 65 years, the southern sea otter is gradually reoccupying areas where once it flourished. As it reestablishes itself in former habitats, the otter forages upon a large number and variety of marine organisms, limiting the abundance and sizes of some, augmenting the growth and distribution of others. Its profound effects on algal productivity and on the structural relationships within kelp forests and other communities it reoccupies along the California coast are exceedingly complex. Only a hint of their intricacies and dynamics have emerged so far.

Observations by Lowry and Pearse (1973), in a rich and varied kelp forest off Pacific Grove, where large numbers of otters have foraged heavily for more than ten years, suggest that as a result of preying upon algal grazers — such as sea urchins, kelp crabs, abalones, and snails — sea otters enhance primary production by benthic algae. Kelp forests, which grow at a phenomenal rate, are among the most productive habitats on earth. They supply nutrition to their occupants at a level of production equal to sugar cane and twice that of corn — with giant kelp in Monterey Bay yielding twenty-four tons of organic matter a year per acre.

The enhancement of such kelp forests leads to a particularly rich assortment of resident plants and animals. In the forest studied by Lowry and Pearse, eighty species of algae, three-hundred species of macro-invertebrates, and sixty species of fish were noted. Such species diversity lends resiliency and stability to an ecosystem, dampening the amplitude of possible natural or unnatural oscillations and buffering against catastrophic change. Enhanced kelp production results not only in increased shelter and nourishment for the many animals within the forest, but also leads to an increase in algal debris and detritus which drifts out to supply food for faunal communities far removed. Sea otters, therefore, appear to play a beneficial role in maximizing the biotic potential and increasing the stability of kelp communities.

From Alaska ... come similar findings. Estes and Palmisano (1974), working in nearshore and intertidal waters, with and without sea otters, in the Rat and Near Island groups of the Aleutian archipelago, have convincingly clarified and corroborated the power role otters play in structuring nearshore communities. They found dense kelp beds and a rich associated community at Amchitka, where there were about 60 otters per square mile; they found sparse, scattered kelp, a dense carpet of large sea urchins, and a significant reduction in community diversity at Attu and Shemya where otters were scarce or absent. From this they conclude that the sea otter is a keystone species, important in determining structures and dynamic relations within nearshore communities, and that it is an evolutionary component essential to the integrity and stability of the ecosystem.

Later on in her article Dr. Davis explains:

The effects of the maritime fur rush resulted in more than the near annihilation of a unique mammal. It caused the disruption of a marine equilibrium that had evolved over millions of years. In the absence of this primary predator, which had played an important regulatory role in the marine community over a vast period of time, significant changes took place. Various large grazers and filter feeders such as urchins, abalones, mussels, clams, crabs, and barnacles now reached high densities, monopolizing space and food previously available to a variety of other organisms. Overall species diversity was affected and a secondary kind of faunal association and equilibrium evolved. The shellfisheries coveted and exploited by modern man were thus born.

With time, man increased his numbers, his effects on the marine environment, his taste for shellfish, and his expertise for invading subtidal coast waters.

Of course, this situation was an aberration. When the Chinese, then the Japanese, came to California after the mid-1800s, abalone (presumably lobsters, too) were abundant along the intertide of the continental shelf as well as in the Channel Islands. When the Caucasians entered the abalone trade toward the end of the 1920s they found bonanzas yet untouched by the limited industry that California's Orientals managed.

So, it would seem natural for all of these fishermen, Caucasian and Oriental, to assume that this unnatural state was natural. And, it was natural for them not to reason that nature had lost her equilibrium for a time. Dr. Davis points to one obvious example of the result of an unwittingly manmade alteration in the marine environment during the 1960s off southern California:

Eventually, in certain areas, the new, otterless ecosystem was upset by a combination of human-induced and natural circumstances. Off southern California, in the absence of a primary predator with varied appetite (the otter) and under heavy pressure from a new predator with selective tastes (man), delectables such as abalones and lobsters were harvested in great numbers and sea urchins were left to multiply and to occupy ecosystem vacancies.

Nourished by an ocean discharge of sewage effluent and abetted by several warm-water years, the already enlarged and unregulated urchin population began grazing out of control. Once-lush kelp forests were soon destroyed, depriving the remaining abalones, lobsters, and many other sea creatures of the shelter and sustaining environment necessary in which to thrive or even survive... Similar, or other types, of upsets may happen in the future as sea urchins continue to usurp abalone spaces and encroach upon kelp forests. Or as man, in a newly-created urchin fishery, quickly harvests vast quantities of this spiny animal to send to Japan, leaving little chance for kelp community adjustments to occur, or for reserves of a prime food item to remain for otters as they forage along the coast.

There is no possibility of returning to former ecosystems, naturally. One can never go back and nothing is static. As Dr. Davis says, otter and shellfish once flourished along our rugged Pacific shoreline. However (she continues):

Today the situation has changed. There are fewer otter, fewer abalones, and many, many more men ... Man changed things drastically when he removed the otter, and is altering the situation again as he over-exploits the shellfisheries. In the southern sea otter's renewed and expanding realm of influence, however, it appears that natural conditions are being restored and the equation is being balanced. . .

Dr. Davis continues:

Recurrent plans to restrict a remnant and threatened natural marine predator — the otter — to save diminishing shellfisheries for humans might work for a moment in time, but will prove fruitless unless man learns to regulate himself. The depleted state of many shellfisheries far outside the otter's present range in California, and elsewhere along our country's

FOLDED SANDSTONE creates habitat for abalone, urchins, crabs and other invertebrate favorites of the sea otter. (Jane H. Bailey Photo)

coastlines, give little evidence that man has learned this lesson so far.

In any event, there are certain important tradeoffs to consider. From the economic viewpoint, although certain shellfisheries eventually may be reduced to levels sustainable only to otters, kelp production — on which a substantial industry, and other kelp-dependent fisheries are based — will be enhanced. Scientifically speaking, the opportunity to observe and document the complex and long-term effects of a primary predator as it reclaims former habitat and helps to restore the integrity of an ecosystem impacted by man is simply unparalleled.

From a biological perspective, the otter is a natural member of the marine community subject to natural law, an important evolutionary component of the nearshore environment that is re-establishing itself in its former realm. The otter should not be restricted in range, nor should it be limited in numbers, before optimum population levels are reached and its profound influences on the marine environment are understood.[10]

TWENTY-FIVE

Why The Reduced Shellfish Resources?

FORAGERS figure in the second major difference of opinion, that of where to place the blame for the reduction of shellfish in certain areas, or the reduced takes for certain pickers. The Department of Fish and Game agrees that the landings of shellfish have decreased in magnitude with the increase in both sport and commercial human foragers. Presumably these foragers also agree. The classic example is the leaping increase in licensed commercial abalone fishermen in California from eleven in 1928 to five hundred and five in 1963.

In 1963, as a result of the onset of complaints by the abalone fishermen of San Luis Obispo County that the otters were invading the resource of their area (in particular the Estero Point red beds) a state Senate fact-finding committee on natural resources held a hearing in the county seat of San Luis Obispo.

Official Department of Fish and Game studies made the previous year indicated that:

> Twenty miles of coastline below San Simeon which formerly produced abalone year after year under continuous commercial exploitation has been completely ruined for abalone as a result of the southern migration of the California herds. It has nothing to do with the number of divers now working, because the otters take the entire population, not just those of legal size. The fact is that otters, urchins, and abalones do not coexist and the entire commercial abalone fishery is very seriously threatened by possible southern expansion of range.[4]

In another study K. W. Cox, who authored for the Department the abalone bulletin Number 118, 1962, reported to the Senate committee:

> In 1956 we went into Shelter Cove right off Monterey and over a period of several days tagged 513 abalone. One year later we came back in the area and we spent approximately three days searching and we found five abalone... one of which had a tag. The area where we were able to collect five hundred abalone in an hour we couldn't find any.
>
> On one dive I brought up over two dozen broken shells... characteristic of broken ones of the sea otters. We were told... by the caretaker, that a herd of sea otters had spent the winter in this cove... I had been called to task for not reporting this... However, I felt that this was not an adequate experiment.[4]

The deputy director of the Department, Harry Anderson, at that time (the report continued):

> ...compared commercial landings of abalones in certain areas before and after sea otters were present in these areas. In 1961 when sea otters were present 'the catch was over 1,550,000 pounds, by far the largest catch of any year in the 10-year period'. He indicated further that competition among abalone fishermen has increased greatly. Since the abalone resource is limited, it becomes apparent that the individual fisherman can expect to obtain fewer abalones than when competition among them was less. It was concluded that 'all the evidence we have indicates that the sea otter has not seriously harmed or threatened the abalone resource'.[4]

The matter was laid to rest officially, with the hearing's conclusion that "...all the evidence we have indicates that the sea otter has not seriously harmed or threatened the abalone resource".[4]

In retrospect it is difficult for most observers to fathom the outcome of the hearing in the face of such damning evidence for the prosecution. Understandably, the frustration was great among the abalone harvesters of San Luis Obispo County. One must remember that the otter had no organized lobby at that time, 1963, and at that juncture there may have been no one speaking up to influence the

SHEEPHEAD and other fish feed on abalone flipped over by the surge of winter storms. (California DFG Photo)

Department's program management plan on Enhydra's behalf. This means that the determination on the Committee's part to allow the status quo was almost certain to have been a result of facts and opinion from the combination of the Department and the abalone pickers, sport and commercial.

But the controversy continued: the abalone divers and boat owners working the Pt. Estero red beds continued complaining and the Department's hands were tied without either orders or sanction from the Legislature to act. The fishermen continued bringing evidence to the long-since cognizant Department in both the field and at headquarters: exhibits of abalone shells with the crown fractured by the otter's pounding them with his rock tool to release the mollusk's grip on his reef. Incidentally, long before a diver observed an otter at this trick, the divers concluded that Enhydra preyed on the well-anchored giant snail.

At this juncture some sportsmen commenced predicting the otter's entry into the Pismo Beach clam beds and cooperated to warn the Department through petitions scattered throughout the county's sports stores and those retail shops selling state fishing licenses.

By the mid-1960s the otter had not traveled much farther to the north of his range, but his scouts had reached Pt. Estero and the *Haliotis rufescens*, or red abalone, fisheries so cherished by the sport and commercial fishermen. By then he had decimated the Beckett's Reef fishery, traditionally a rich source for commercial vessels.

One well-established diver, boat owner, and processor took another, a practical, tack by commencing to research raising abalone in the laboratory, nursery style. Such was one man's patience and long view.

In 1968 the Legislature authorized a three-year study of the California otter by the Department. Two years later the Department's Director, E. C. Fullerton, announced that his agency had no intention of making any recommendation to the solons on a new bill to manage the otter until this study was completed: "The more we know about the otter, the more we realize that we know very little. We want to re-trench and see if what we are doing so far is right. We've got to go back and learn more."

An honest statement, it may have been an understatement, too. Surely the United States Fish and Wildlife Service biologists and

WELL-CAMOUFLAGED abalones *(Haliotis rufescens)* cluster in a reef crevice. (Glen Bickford Photo)

everyone concerned with them as they studied the otter in the Aleutians from 1954 to 1968 would heartily agree. One would think upon reading Dr. Ķenyon's comprehensive volume that there could be nothing that Enhydra had, physically or psychologically, to hide from those thorough scientists and their field assistants. Apparently this is not the case. For purposes of moving and protecting the otter, specifically the California branch, a great deal of information remains to be collected on behavior, distribution, longevity, population dynamics, mortality, feeding habits, the effects of Enhydra on the kelp ecology, taxonomy, physiology, and more.

By 1968 the southern sea otter numbered 1014, and the following year brought a second and more emotional collision of both factions: the otter's champions and the abalone divers (with the commercial divers more prominent in the arena than the sport pickers). State Senator Alan R. Grunsky, representing both counties whose shores were home to the otter (and Santa Cruz county which Enhydra would reach later), designed Bill SB 442. This would allow the removal of otters wandering beyond the otter refuge delineated by the state in 1959.

Senate Bill 442

> Provides that sea otters may be taken outside the California Sea Otter Refuge under a permit or by the Department of Fish and Game, providing there has been a public hearing by the Fish and Game Commission, which has been given no less than 30 days notice, and there has been a specific finding by the commission that this action will not endanger the sea otter resource. Prohibits both sports and commercial taking of abalone from the refuge area.

The hearing on this measure before the Committee on Natural Resources was the initial major endeavor of the newly organized Friends of the Sea Otter. Busloads of its young and its adult members converged on the state capitol and convened in the hearing room. Both sport and commercial interests came to witness, although few of them. This was understandable: public interest lobbying in respect to ecological issues was in its infancy. Legislature, Department, Fish & Game Commission — these were the traditional patrons, guardians, decisionmakers.

The Friends of the Sea Otter carried the day. They bore petitions signed by 14,884 Californians (and again that many submitted later following the hearing — all gathered in a fortnight). But, of course, the otter lobby's success was not a result of the force of their numbers present. It was the weight of their testimony. They were prepared with arguments garnered by study, by research including the consultation of authorities in the fields of marine biology, zoology, and resource management. In the leadership's terms, the victory was laid to "authoritative scientific minds and a broad expanse of citizens' sentiment".[11, 12]

The SB 442 read like this eventually:

Amended

Provides that sea otters may be pursued, caught, or captured, but not killed or destroyed, by the Department of Fish & Game outside the California Sea Otter Refuge, for scientific or propagation purposes or to prevent conflict with other marine resources provided that there has been a public hearing by the Fish & Game Commission, which has been given no less than 30 days notice, and there has been a specific finding by the commission that this action will not endanger the sea otter resource. Prohibits both sport and commercial taking of abalone from the refuge area.

On April 13, 1970, the Sierra Club made its view known on the question by a resolution:

Sierra Club Resolution

The Sierra Club opposes the intent of SB 442, currently pending before the California State Senate, which would authorize the transplantation of sea otters found outside of the California Sea Otter Refuge. The tolerances of sea otters to reestablishment in cold Pacific Northwest water has not been sufficiently studied, and mass transplantation may well result in the needless destruction of hundreds of these rare animals.

We further recommend that a technical commission be appointed to conduct an in-depth study of all marine resources along the Coast, including environmental hazards as well as measures to protect a balanced ecology in which both the sea otter and the abalone will be enhanced and preserved. This study should be carried out by an institution of recognized competence and impartiality to resist pressures originating from narrow viewpoints.

The result was that SB 442 returned to Committee for further study in preparation for the 1971 session of the Legislature, while the fishing people resigned themselves to the loss of the long-prolific red beds off Estero Point and Cambria. In addition, more of the Morro Bay based commercial abalone boats, divers and crews followed their former colleagues to Santa Barbara where the beds off of the Channel Islands remained in healthy condition, with no threat from the otter in the near future.

The end of 1974 brought the Department's keenly awaited report on the otter to the public and the Legislature: A REPORT ON THE SOUTHERN SEA OTTER IN CALIFORNIA, Marine Resources Technical Report #20. And it blew the whistle on the otter in no uncertain terms.

The report was the reply to arguments Number One and Number Two. Then, on the heels of Report #20 came an equally devastating report nailing down the argument over the ravages wrought on the clam population where the little mammal worked and played: the entirety of his range, from the foot of Estero Bay north to the extreme of Monterey Bay.

TWENTY-SIX

In The Event Of A Catastrophe

TWO additional and vital questions confront those people concerned over the sea otter. The first, whether or not a catastrophic loss of otters from an oil spill, by seawater contaminated by toxicants, or other causes can be replaced with the northern species, or branch, of the mammal.

The second, whether or not to remove otters from their wild habitat to a captive one in aquaria, zoos, marine institutions, either public or private.

The first question hinges upon whether or not the southerner, Enhydra lutris nereis is a subspecies, or in fact a member of the northern species, Enhydra lutris lutris. The bearing it has on Number One is this: one does not have to be a purist or an environmentalist to reject the annihilation of an animal species. If it is true that Enhydra lutris nereis is indeed a subspecies, then many would insist that all threats to its collective life be removed.

Many, many others point to the abundance of Enhydra lutris lutris up north: between 100,000 and 140,000. It has been common knowledge that much starvation among certain colonies there has resulted from outgrowing their environment's capacity to support them. Indeed, in 1969 the state of Alaska culled many for the purpose of reopening the otter fur commerce. So, these folks opt to protect all of those prey items that they themselves and the otters fancy — or, on which their livelihood depends.

The otter's side agrees with the opinion offered by Professor Aryan I. Roest, head of the department of biology at the California Polytechnic State University of San Luis Obispo. After a comparative study of northern and southern otters, the professor concluded: "The subspecies Enhydra lutris nereis is . . .considered valid as the proper designation of the southern sea otter along the California coast".[13]

Due to the sedentary habits of the otter and its originally vast range of six thousand miles from the Kurile Islands to Baja California's midsection, Roest pointed out that one would expect local races or subspecies to have developed. He found four skull measurements to be of taxonomic value. Using these, he was able to identify correctly 90.5% as Californian. He also called attention to the sea otter's size, smaller than the northerner's.

As for the estimate of whether or not there are sufficient members of the southern branch that it can afford to expend some of the members, the Fish and Game Department of California has officially announced that it believes the southern species is populous enough that it should not be included in the endangered species category, which indeed excluded it from the Department's 1971 endangered species list.

To others, the few differences in conformation of the skull, together with the small size difference between the two otter branches, are not sufficiently important to weight the scales in such an important issue as preserving more invertebrates for either recreation or commercial harvesting purposes.

This recalls another campaign undertaken by the Friends of the Sea Otter organization: the petitions with 65,000 signatures of their friends — together with the Sierra Club — rained upon the Department of the Interior between November, 1976, and February 1977, to influence the agency to restore the otter to the e.s. status. The result was almost as desired: effective February 11, 1977, the southern otter was placed in the threatened species category.

Lastly: the subject of placing otters in captivity. Learning to capture, to hold, and to transplant (now called translocation) has cost dearly in otter lives, and the procedure may still be far from beaten into a safe one. California's Department of Fish and Game can go to school on the experience of the United States Fish and Wildlife Service between 1950 and 1965, and Alaska's more recent experience translocating otters to Washington and Oregon.

Attempting to fulfill its mission to revive the trade in otter pelts, the federal agency lost more otters than it succeeded in transplanting to the tribe's former habitats in the northeastern Pacific. Both to relieve the population pressure in nearshore ecosystems of certain of the Aleutian Islands contributing to winter die-offs and to repopulate former habitats the USFWS had to grope along by trial and error. The department even delved into the limited literature available on Russian experiments in a like endeavor.

The experiments in moving the otter offered a deeper understanding of the baffling psyche of a baffling mammal, as the men witnessed their traumatic effect on those highstrung creatures undergoing the move and on the survivors, few that there were.

Dr. Kenyon[4] reported the project's coming to a standstill until the biologists, zoologists, and their field workers could learn more about the otter (presumably, the whole otter).

First lesson: to hold otters on land they need circulating fresh air and a pool of either circulating saltwater or circulating fresh water (or water cleaned or replaced daily or more often). Because Enhydra eats lying on his back and because he must continually shake or wash the crumbs from his fur dining table, he should eat in the water. Because his fur must be spotlessly clean for his survival, he must have water which is free of his body waste and food remnants. Because of his lack of a thermostat, he must be able to cool his body, taking frequent dips to accomplish this unless he is in the sea.

An early and costly lesson was that transporting on dry bedding (straw, etc.) is a mistake; it becomes soiled and in turn soils the pelage. When the otters were turned from the boat into their new home in the sea, they left a wake of dirty water behind and obviously were instantaneously chilled. Hurriedly several were pulled from the sea, wet to the skin and rigid from the cold, near death. Presumably none of the otters survived this trial. Yet, paradoxically, the otter can live in seas surrounded by ice; many have lived as far north as the pack ice region.

Lesson Number One, then was that the fur loses its impermeability if soiled, and the litter serving as bedding for the mammal becomes soiled enroute to the destination. Another lesson: this method can succeed if the journey is a brief one and if the otter is watched closely enough to be kept clean.

Aerial translocation is the superior method, discovered at the expense of many more otter lives. The flight must be short unless it is in an unheated plane with attendants to cool the animals frequently. An experiment by the State of Alaska in flying otters tranquilized also wasted lives. However, much time and experience has passed since then, 1965, and both tranquilizers and other accommodations doubtless have been improved sufficiently to warrant near-repetition. The California Department of Fish and Game flew those stranded otters to the San Diego Sea World during the mid-1970s, and with success.

In effect, to fly the otters requires most fastidiously detailed care and nurture to prevent the onset of heat stress, one of the otter's principal enemies.

At long last the formula for success was refined to perfection as far as flying was concerned: an unheated cabin with attendants to cool the animals with ice and water during the entire flight. It is difficult to believe that the welfare of a lower animal could be such a challenge for man.

In 1967 a few men from Seattle were given permission to remove a half-dozen otters from the Aleutians and install them in their city's Woodland Park zoo. The hunters predicted hardships for themselves, but the vicissitudes they experienced were unforeseen. And, they had studied and consulted authories well in advance of the hunt to avoid affronting the quarry, if possible.

Oversized butterfly nets were the tools for snaring, and the men were reasonably certain that they would stay high and dry as they plucked the otters from the beaches with the utmost delicacy and tact in consideration of their emotions. In fact, with the combination of this deference and the foul weather, all of the men fell ill. One man collapsed on the beach following a week of wading in freezing shallows, creeping over slick rocks coated with slippery sea lettuce.

Occasionally the hunters received a nip through their multi-layered clothing and boots. Otter mothers were especially vehement, frantic over the wellbeing of their offspring. Two of the safari men or their assistants would carry a single otter over five miles of tundra to holding tanks. After a few days in these (and according to their rulebook) the Seattle hunters moved their catch to the plane via mattress-padded trucks. During all of the surface travel the otters were up-tight, tense, nervous — in fact it was not until they were airborne and beyond the scent and sound of their sea and islet that the kidnaped otters relaxed, turning to face the next episode of their adventure.

During the ten-hour flight the men splashed seawater over their captives and poured glass after glass of fresh water directly into the mouth of each. The cabin temperature was uncomfortably low for the human passengers but suited the mammals, and ice surrounding the cages in canvas bags offered them additional comfort assurance.

The success of the safari was a feat even at the late date of 1967, but the combined services it required for its success were a shocker:

CAPTIVE ADULT male otters of group brought from Amchitka Is-lands. Pups remain with mother a year, apprenticing in survival tactics. (Karl W. Kenyon Photo, Bureau of Sport Fisheries & Wildlife)

veterinarians, biologists, two airlines, a fire department, the USFWS, the U.S. Atomic Energy Commission, and the Alaskan government — all in synchronized concert.

These hard-earned rules for translocation concern the northern branch of the family. Once upon a time one could have assumed that an otter is an otter. Today the otter book of knowledge is filling rapidly and perhaps quite a distinct book of rules will be written soon solely on the California otter.

In early 1974 the California Department of Fish and Game proposed stocking some of the aquaria around the world with California otters to relieve pressures on our shoreline ecosystem and to establish seed pools for replenishing pods decimated or destroyed by disasters.

In the happy event that the otter might reproduce successfully in captivity, the Department must have believed that succeeding generations reared in captivity could adapt to nature's raw world. The otter's champions' reply is to claim that this would pose a great gamble even for a hardier animal, one with a tougher constitution and temperament than that of the otter. Also, in their opinion, if this plan materialized it would mean initially moving a couple of hundred of the mammals by the most expensive means: airplanes with attendant nurturers.

The plan assumes that many aquaria would accept an otter or multiple otters. Its opponents claim that it is such a steep challenge for an aquarium to keep an otter healthy that there may be few offers to host an otter. Moreover, the zoo director who said that the otter eats more than a lion and costs more to feed than an elephant may exaggerate very little, if at all. For, Enhydra's appetite for budget-shattering dishes such as clam, squid, octopus, crab, red snapper, urchin, in quantity can make zoo authorities spending their taxpayers' money wary of assuming his support.

In the late 1960s Woodland Park's otter budget was five dollars per day per otter to support them in the manner to which they were accustomed. And that was a day when prices of clam, squid, crab, snapper, etc., were far less inflated than today's prices: $2.50. $.80, $7.80, $1.80, etc.

Four adult otters, captives at San Diego's Sea World together consumed eighty pounds of clams and between fifteen and twenty pounds

CRAB FOR LUNCH is enjoyed by one of a family of four Aleutian Island otters living in the Seattle Aquarium in 1978. (Seattle Aquarium Photo)

of crabs in 1972. A private aquarium's income exceeds that of most municipal zoos and aquaria, and the latter far outnumber the former. Perhaps this, too, narrows down the number of hosts available to accept surplus otters.

In the last analysis perhaps doling out the excess otters to zoos rests as the business world puts it: on the question of cost-benefit. Perhaps the stunning and fascinating — even luxurious — educational institution, the Seattle Municipal Aquarium on the wharf, may be a harbinger of the creative public aquarium.

Whatever its budget source, it appears ample for a continuously growing series of live faunal exhibits, live and apparently thriving in the innovative and wide-ranging habitats that it shelters.

However, circumstances bringing such an establishment into being and maintaining it may be few and far between. To duplicate Seattle's aquarium would be a challenge that few municipalities could assume. Perhaps only private aquaria which can command handsome entrance fees will be able to assume the steep costs necessary to finance designers, builders, marine scientists, maintenance, feed bills, on so grand a scale as that of Seattle, Sea World, or Marineland.

In 1974 a biologist and member of the federal Marine Mammal Commission (guardians of the otter) said that he believed that only four or five aquaria in the United States will be able to equal Sea World's expensive otter display, and that the Commission would accept only aquaria of equal quality.

So, say the otter's friends, this would indicate pitifully few homes for excess sea otters, and they spurn the suggestion as a part of the solution.

TWENTY-SEVEN

Officialdom Blows The Whistle

In 1974 the California Department of Fish and Game had studied the California sea otter for five years to the extent of its capacity vis a vis the resources available to it (funds, equipment, manpower, etc.). Begun before the state's guardianship role was transferred to the federal government, the information sought was long overdue as guidance in the future management of the otter and the shellfish resources.

Rather than paraphrase this report, actual excerpts drawn directly from it follow:

> This report discusses in detail findings and observations of 5 years of research on the sea otter population and its relationship to the nearshore marine evironment in California. Initial efforts were directed at providing some relief to the commercial abalone fishery in the Cambria-Point Estero area north of Morro Bay. This fishery has subsequently collapsed along with other commercial and sport abalone and sport crab fisheries throughout the sea otter's range due to continued sea otter foraging.
>
> Capturing, tagging and translocation studies, censusing studies, examination of sea otter remains, habitat surveys, food habits observations and studies on otters in captivity provide a broad base of information on the expanding sea otter population in California and its effects on resources utilized by man.

Recommendations for sea otter management consistent with esthetic, recreational, and commercial uses of marine resources are included in this report.

Foreword to MTR #20

The Department of Fish and Game Sea Otter Research Project was inititated in July, 1968, in response to recommendations in a report presented to the Legislature in January, 1968. The report, requested by Senate Concurrent Resolution No. 74, 1967 Legislative Session, was entitled *Report on the Sea Otter, Abalone and Kelp Resources in San Luis Obispo and Monterey Counties and Proposals for Reducing the Conflict Between the Commercial Abalone Industry and the Sea Otter* (Bissell and Hubbard, 1968). . ."

The report established the guidelines and direction for the Sea Otter Research Project. A two-phase approach was recommended consisting of an initial three-year phase to gather information necessary for confident, safe management of the sea otter and to provide a measure of relief to the commercial abalone fishery; and a subsequent continuing phase based largely on information gained during the first phase.

In the interim, federal legislation, resulting in the Marine Mammals Protection Act of 1972, has placed sea otters under the jurisdiction of the U.S. Department of Interior. This federal legislation precluded the state from implementing management of sea otters, and trapping and tagging operations in progress were terminated on December 21, 1972, the effective date of the Marine Mammals Protection Act. Implementation of a management plan for sea otters and continuation of research now depends on obtaining a permit from the Department of Interior.

This report contains results of the project's research activities and management recommendations for sea otters consistent with beneficial uses of living marine resources.

Introduction to MTR #20

...Due to extensive unregulated harvesting, sea otter populations declined to low levels throughout their range by the mid 1800's and the species was nearly extinct in California at the turn of the Twentieth Century.

Protection was provided sea otters by the International Fur Seal Treaty of 1911 which prohibited the taking of sea otters and fur seals. California laws prohibiting taking or possessing sea otters or their skins have been in effect since 1913. As further protecton against shooting, the California Sea Otter Game Refuge was established in 1941; possession of firearms is prohibited within the Refuge. Initially the Refuge included the portions of Monterey County lying west on Highway 1 between Malpaso Creek and Swiss Canyon Arroyo and between Castro Canyon and Dolan Creek (Figure 1). In 1959 the Sea Otter Game Refuge was expanded to include all that land lying west of Highway 1 between the Carmel River on the north and Santa Rosa Creek at Cambria on the south.

...Based on recent observations, the population now ranges from the vicinity of Santa Cruz, Santa Cruz County, to the vicinity of Point Buchon, San Luis Obispo County (Figure 2).

As the sea otters increased in numbers and extended their range, a resource conflict developed between abalone fishermen and the sea otter in the commercial abalone beds from Cape San Martin to Cayucos. Examination of sport and commercial abalone catch records and fishery history in context with the sea otter's expanding range documents this conflict. The result has been that extensive sport and commercial abalone fisheries and sport rock crab fisheries have virtually disappeared in the wake of the expanding sea otter population. Concern over these and other mounting problems prompted the Department of Fish and Game's research on the sea otter population and related problems.

In this report, we have attempted to provide information on the sea otter population and present and potential resource use problems as well as to provide the basis for a rational solution to these problems which will assure the continuation of a healthy sea otter population along the California coast.

The Conclusions of the Report MTR #20

Emphasis in the early phase of the Sea Otter Research Project was directed toward development of trapping and tagging gear and gaining experience in handling sea otters. Initial capturing efforts utilized gill nets which worked well, but resulted in a few sea otter drownings. Mortality levels due to trapping during early project activities had no adverse effects on the sea otter population. However, these activities were curtailed and efforts were redirected to developing a safe, efficient capture technique. The result was a diver-held capture device which has eliminated capture mortality.

Fifty-eight sea otters were captured during the 5 years of this study, 29 with gill nets and 29 with the diver-held capture device. Seventeen were translocated within the range, tagged, released; 29 were tagged and released on site; 8 were placed in captivity; 4 drowned in the nets.

In all, 23 sea otters were removed from the Cambria-Point Estero area by translocation, placing otters in captivity, and capture mortality. The removal of otters from this area, designed to provide some relief to the commercial abalone fishery was unsuccessful due to the return of some translocated otters and the continued natural influx of additional otters into the area. As the sea otter population continued to extend its range to the south, the commercial abalone fishery north of Morro Bay completely collapsed. Sea otters foraged so heavily on abalones in this area that by 1971 abalone divers abandoned the last of the historically abundant abalone beds north of Point Estero that had supported an annual commercial harvest for many years. The sport abalone fishery within the sea otter's range from Monterey to Cayucos has been similarly affected.

Translocation of otters outside the sea otter's range was investigated as a possible solution to resource use problems. Suitable sea otter habitat exists along much of the California coast. However, due to the extreme potential for additional resource use conflicts with a variety of resources wherever such habitat exists, translocation outside the present range is not a feasible solution to current problems.

Sonic barriers are not considered a feasible method to limit sea otter range expansion.

Aerial and surface censuses have revealed that the sea otter population is continuing to increase in numbers and expand its range. These censuses provide the basis for population estimates and density calculations. The sea otter population in mid-1973 was estimated at about 1,600 to 1,800 animals and ranged from Santa Cruz on the north to just beyond Point Buchon on the south.

The sea otter population, as a whole, apparently has been increasing at a faster rate than the segment within a major central portion of the range. The data indicate that the excess has been supporting range expansion with significantly greater densities of sea otters occurring at the extremes of the range.

Range expansion is apparently accomplished largely by accumulating of subadult and younger adult animals at the fringes of the range.

Capture data reveal that sea otters in California segregate by sex much as they do in populations in the north Pacific. The data suggest that males may have a larger home range than females, as is reported for northern populations, but more information is needed to establish home range in California.

Little information is available about sex and age groupings and movements throughout a major central portion of the range.

Sea otter carcasses have been recovered primarily toward the ends of the range. Cause of death in sea otters in California in recent years has been found to be due to a variety of human and natural causes. Human causes of sea otter deaths have included being hit by boats, shooting or spearing, and blows. Boating accidents appear to be he most common human caused mortality. Several animals were definitely shot in 1969 and 1970, but shooting has not been much a problem since. Natural deaths occur from a variety of causes such as infection, trauma, starvation, etc. A significant increase in natural mortality occurred during the 1972-1973 winter-spring period. This was apparently associated with a relatively severe winter, combined with concentrations of animals in certain areas with resultant depletion of food supplies. A higher ratio of pups, subadults, and aged adults to adults was apparent in this die-off compared to prior years. Animals in these age groups are apparently less able to forage as efficiently under such conditions.

Sea otter carcass materials have been provided to a number of scientific and educational institutions for studies on taxonomy anatomy and physiology, environmental contaminants such as pesticides, polychlorinated biphenyls and trace and major elements and studies of parasites.

Habitat studies within the sea otter's range reveal that sea otters exert a profound effect on the nearshore environment, particularly on biological community structures of nearshore invertebrates. Habitat studies adjacent to the sea otter's range indicate that these areas will support sea otter population expansion.

Food habits studies reveal considerable variation in the sea otter's diet depending on the location and the length of time otters have been in an area. In newly colonized areas where sea urchins, abalones and crabs are abundant, these have been observed to constitute a major portion of the diet. As these become depleted with continued foraging, the diet becomes more diverse and less prefered forage items become more significant to the diet. Human utilization of many sea otter forage items virtually ceases in the presence of significant numbers of foraging otters as forage items become reduced in number and size and are restricted to rocky crevices and other protected habitat.

Successful long-term sustenance of sea otters in captivity in Washington State has demonstrated that sea otters can be successfuly maintained in captivity. Early in our operations, two sea otters were maintained in captivity at Stanford Research Institute's Biological Sonar Laboratory for nearly 8 months for tagging and other studies. An opportunity to further our knowledge of the sea otter's behavior, food habits, physiology, medical care, etc., is now possible through captive studies being developed on four sea otters placed in captivity at Sea World, San Diego, in December 1972. This information should help to assure that a healthy sea otter population will be maintained off our coast.

Population dynamics data, habitat surveys, and food habits studies all indicate that the sea otter population in California is continuing to increase in numbers and expand its range. These studies also indicate that the sea otter is directly responsible for the loss of sport and commercial abalone and sport crab fisheries within the sea otter's range. If it were feasible to remove sea otters and prevent them from re-entering abalone beds, the now defunct abalone fishery north of Point Estero could most likely be returned to its former production level. If otters were removed from the Point Buchon area, the remaining sport and commercial red abalone fisheries, the developing sea urchin fishery and crab fisheries there could be saved.

However, if unrestricted expansion of sea otters is allowed to occur in California, additional sport and commercial resources currently being utilized by man will be adversely affected. Southward range expansion will bring otters into conflict with fisheries for pink and green abalones, Pismo and other clams, crabs and lobsters. Northward range expansion, already begun, will conflict with sport and commercial abalone and crab fisheries along the Santa Cruz-San Mateo coast and, eventually, abalone, crab, scallop and clam fisheries and possibly oyster farming on the north coast.

Since translocation of sea otters outside the present range in California would only compound the problems, the only practical way to provide for continued human utilization of resources foraged upon by sea otters and also maintain a healthy population of sea otters in California, is to manage a portion of the coast for sea otters and limit their range to that area and to continue to manage other coastal areas for human resource usage.

Recommendations

...Research has...demonstrated that two basic alternatives are available for maintaining the California sea otter resource: Protection and management of a healthy sea otter population restricted within geographical limits along the California coast (and) protection of a unrestricted sea otter population along the California coast.

We recommend against the second management alternative... Research has demonstrated the many valuable marine invertebrates cannot coexist with sea otters in numbers and sizes that can be utilized by man. Therefore, to follow this alternative would mean that human use of a variety of living marine resources would be sacrificed, in addition to those already lost, to sustain the expanding sea otter population.

If the alternative of not restricting the expansion of the sea otter population is selected, then the Department's continuing activities should be limited to sporadic surveillance and censusing of the population.

Management and restriction of the sea otter population within its present range in California would provide protection for a variety of resource uses adjacent to the sea otter's range. Implementation of restriction would probably be facilitated by establishing boundaries for management in the vicinity of long stretches of sandy beaches and sandy benthic habit offshore. Although sea otters forage over sandy areas devoid of rocky reef-kelp bed habitat, they have not been observed to establish rafting groups in such areas. In addition, long stretches of sandy beaches and sandy offshore habitat such as occur along Monterey Bay appear to provide partial barriers to range expansion.

Therefore, if resource uses adjacent to the present sea otter's range are to be protected from sea otter foraging, it is recommended that:

1. The sea otter's range be restricted in the coastal area between Moss Landing, Monterey County, and Morro Bay, San Luis Obispo County. These boundaries would allow for some sandy foraging habitat adjacent to the last rafting habitat at the extremes of the recommended area. Establishment of a southern boundary in the vicinity of Avila (near the long stretch of sandy habitat along Pismo Beach) would adversely affect fisheries for abalones, crabs, and sea urchins from Morro Bay to Avila and would present a high risk for potential damage to the important Pismo clam sportfishery along Pismo Beach.

2. A program be developed which will restrict sea otters to the recommended area.

3. Biological studies be designed and conducted concurrently to determine the progress and success of the management activities. These studies should provide that:

a. High priority be given to obtaining much needed additional sea otter population dynamics information. Such information must include additional data on birth and death rates, sex ratios, age composition, distribution and movements throughout the population. Much of this information can only be obtained by tagging animals throughout the range. It may be necessary to tag at least 10% or more of the population to obtain statistically significant data.

b. Further ecological studies be conducted throughout the range. Such studies should include effects of otters on the nearshore environment in terms of sea otter food resources, effects on kelp bed ecology and characteristics of established sea otter habitat. These studies should be designed to supply information necessary to establish range carrying capacity.

c. Scientific research on sea otters in captivity be continued. Continuing research on captive animals will provide further information on physiology, medical care and husbandry, food habits and behavior.

d. The program of sea otter carcass recovery, processing, and distribution of remains be continued.

e. When adequate information has been accumulated, management recommendations be updated to ensure continuance of a healthy population of sea otters.[1]

TWENTY-EIGHT

— And Once Again Blows The Whistle

ON the heels of the REPORT ON THE SEA OTTER IN CALI-
FORNIA (1974), the Department delivered to the public another
one: PISMO CLAMS AND SEA OTTERS (1975).[14]

The one-two blows from the pair of reports raised the decibel level
of the alarm to a cry-havoc state, the "I told you so's" quadrupled
and rained upon the Department of Fish and Game and presumably
on the source of the Department's orders, the Legislature.

Two sides of the triangle looked to the Department of the Interior
and its Marine Mammal Commission, wishing that they could lever
the Commission into accelerating their decision. Those were the
commercial and the sport pickers.

Would the pioneering otters of the southern frontier arrive at
Pismo Beach before their snail's-paced guardian handed down its
decision on sanctioning California's research project? Finally, would
the permit include permission to capture and remove some, or all,
of the southing rovers?

> Sea otter foraging along Monterey Bay beaches and at Atas-
> cadero State Beach has precluded recreational Pismo clam
> fisheries at six major clamming beaches. Outside the sea ot-
> ter's foraging range Pismo clam stocks are yielding good catches;
> apparently the stringent controls on the recreational fishery is
> adequate to maintain the State's Pismo clam stocks.

This is the introduction to the *abstract* leading into the Marine Resources Technical Report #31, published in 1975 by the California Department of Fish and Game biologists Daniel J. Miller, James E. Hardwick, and Walter A. Dahlstrom: PISMO CLAMS AND SEA OTTERS.

The following are verbatim selections from this report, beginning with the remainder of the abstract.

Clammer interviews at Orange and Los Angeles County beaches and at beaches near Pismo Beach and Morro Bay and in Monterey Bay revealed the clam stocks to be on a healthy, sustainable yield basis. Exceptionally large numbers of small 1.5 to 3.5 inch Pismo clams were reported at all clam beaches surveyed north of Pt. Conception indicating good year class survival in recent years.

Sea otters forage dense Pismo clam beds by moving along a "front" progressively foraging from one beach to the next, reducing the clams to low levels before moving on. Some sea otters continue to forage throughout the areas previously depleted by the larger aggregate moving northward, thus the large numbers of sublegal clams in the 1.5 to 3.5 inch size group in these intertidal and shallow subtidal areas are not expected to reach legal size in numbers sufficient to develop a recreational fishery.

In Monterey Bay about 60,000 Pismo clams were removed or killed by human activity in the April 1974 to March 1975 period. A rough estimate of the Pismo clams consumed by sea otters during this same period in Monterey Bay is over 500,000 clams.

The Report's introduction:

In 1973 sea otters, *Enhydra lutris*, began foraging on Pismo clams, *Tivela stultorum*, in Monterey Bay near Moss Landing and at Atascadero State Beach.   Research personnel at Moss

Landing Marine Laboratories recorded clam densities by means of randomly chosen plots from 1972 to 1974 at Salinas River State Beach (Potrero Road), Smudowski State Beach, and Monterey Bay Academy Beach. During the course of these studies they documented Pismo clam reproduction and densities and the arrival of sea otters in the Potrero Road area in April 1973, and noted subsequent changes in Pismo clam densities. Most striking was the abundance of broken shells on the beach both inter- and subtidally soon after sea otters appeared. By September there were not sufficient clams present for clam reproduction studies at Potrero Road beach. Several more clam density surveys were made in 1974 by Moss Landing Laboratory personnel at Potrero Road beach, Smudowski State Beach, and at Monterey Bay Academy.

In view of the importance of this depletion of Pismo clam stocks by sea otters at this important clamming beach, Department of Fish and Game personnel undertook a search of previously collected data on Pismo clams in Monterey Bay, and initiated collection of several series of data pertaining to sea otter distribution and numbers and effects of sea otter foraging on Pismo clam stocks in Monterey Bay. Additional data were collected on the status of Morro Bay and Pismo Beach Pismo clam stocks in December 1974 and January and February 1975. This report summarizes past data and presents the results of the 1974 . 1975 Monterey Bay and Morro Bay sea otter-Pismo clam interaction studies.

Status of Pismo Clam Stocks
At Major California Beaches

Evaluation of the effects of sea otter foraging on Pismo clams in Monterey Bay requires basic information on the status of clam stocks in Monterey Bay and the possible effects of heavy sport clamming pressure on these stocks. Pismo clam beds in Monterey Bay are at the periphery of clam distribution to the north and a comparison of the fishery and densities in Monterey Bay with comparable data from southern California beaches is essential to fully understand the nature of the relative effects of man and sea otters on clam stocks.

In December 1974 clammer interviews were made at beaches in Monterey Bay and at Morro Bay and Pismo Beach to determine the relative abundance of various sized Pismo clams. In January 1975 an extensive survey was made of clammer effort and catch at Monterey Bay, Morro Bay, and Pismo Beach clam beaches and at certain beaches in Los Angeles and Orange counties.

The initial statewide survey was designed for December; however, exceptionally heavy swells pounded all the beaches from Monterey to Newport in December and abnormally poor conditions prevailed for clamming. Interviews were made in December at Monterey Bay, Morro Bay, and Pismo Beach area beaches, and in spite of the poor conditions there were fair amounts of clams taken at most beaches outside the sea otter's range, but virtually no clams were found at most beaches foraged by sea otters.

Sea otters began foraging along Atascadero State Beach in early 1973 and by fall of 1974 they had reduced the clam stocks to levels below that required to support a recreational fishery... By January 1975 sea otters had not foraged at Morro Spit, but Dick Burge reported substantial foraging of this area starting in late February 1975 as evidenced by presence of broken shells at low tide.

"In the January 23-27, 1975 census excellent clamming conditions prevailed in southern California, fair to poor clamming conditions were present in the Pismo Beach-Morro Bay areas, and fair conditions prevailed in Monterey Bay. Twenty beaches were surveyed during this low tide period. . .

The highest clam-per-hour values were recorded near Newport Pier in Orange County, with high yields also recorded at Huntington Beach, Grand Avenue near Pismo Beach, Morro Spit, and in Monterey Bay at Sunset State Beach, Monterey Bay Academy, and Seacliff State Beach. There are other factors that may result in varying yields between beaches other than poor weather and heavy swells. In Monterey Bay the minimum size limit for Pismo clams is 5 inches... whereas south of Monterey Bay the minimum size limit is 4.5 inches... in greatest shell diameter. There is a closed season from May 1 to September 1 in Monterey Bay, but no closed season to the south. Skindivers commonly take Pismo clams at Pismo Beach but seldom in Monterey Bay. In spite of these differences, clamming success was comparable in intensity and yield throughout the state and there appears to be no serious depletion of stocks, with some limit catches of ten clams per person taken at nearly all clam beaches by experienced clammers even during poor conditions.

The beach area immediately north of Pismo Beach pier shows effects of heavy clamming use more than at other beaches; and low catches were recorded at Bolsa Chica State Beach, but it is not known whether low catches there were due to heavy use or to low natural stocks of clams.

The principle findings of this statewide clammer survey are that Monterey Bay clam stocks outside the sea otter's range were comparable in yield to that of beaches in the center of the Pismo clam range from Pismo Beach to Newport, that clamming effort has not caused depletion of clam stocks in Monterey Bay, and that except possibly for the beach north of Pismo Beach pier, Pismo clam stocks in California appear to be on a healthy sustainable yield outside the sea otter's range...

Even though this one statewide clammer census cannot as yet relate trends, it appears that except for one or two areas clam stocks are withstanding clammer pressure. At Bolsa Chica State Beach there appears to be poor recruitment and at the beach north of Pismo Beach pier low catches of legal sized clams were noted. The low take near Pismo Beach pier is probably due to clammer use, inasmuch as relatively high numbers of sub-legal clams from 3.5 to 4.5 inches were reported by the clammers. Catch-per-hour values increased at Pismo Beach pier from 0.33 clams per hour in December to 0.62 clams per hour in January, but this latter value still represents poor clamming.

MTR #31 continues:

Pismo Clam Mortality in Monterey Bay
Natural and Clamming Mortality

Natural mortality other than by sea otters has not been studied in Monterey Bay, but results of observations by researchers in southern California are probably applicable to this area inasmuch as the same general physical conditions and species of predators are present except for the California corbina, *Menticirrhus undulatus.* Natural predation of small clams can be high as pointed out by Fitch (1950):

'Considering natural mortality it is not probable that more than 200 clams out of 1,000 one- or two-year old clams would ever reach legal size.'

Included in natural mortality of small clams is predation by crabs, bat rays, sharks, and possibly other smaller surf frequenting fishes. Gulls pick up clams left exposed by storms and drop them to break the shell; and there is some predation by the drilling moon snail, *Polinices.* Only a few small Pismo clam shells collected on Monterey Bay beaches contained drill holes. A few gaper shells (halves entire,hinged together and meat gone) were observed, indicating minimal mortality from pollution, killing by hot sun's rays when exposed, or storm damage. Weymouth (1920) described storm damage at Pismo Beach:

'How destructive such changes may be, is seen in some winters when the heavy cutting surf washes out and rolls up the beach such numbers of the clams that windrows are found at high tide line.'

However, Weymouth (1923)   reports these natural disasters are infrequent.

Mortality of clams by man has been of some concern and as was pointed out above stringent legislation has been enacted to lessen mortality of young clams. Massive dieoffs of clams left exposed on the beaches near Pismo Beach were noted by Fitch (1950). Most Pismo clams can eventually rebury themselves, but if the day is hot several hours of exposure out of water can kill them. No such a dieoff has been recorded for Monterey Bay, so possibly temperature conditions were not damaging to exposed clams along Monterey Bay during the days when numbers of these clams may have been left unburied. Fitch (1950) wrote:

> 'In returning clams to deep water the recommended method is to throw the undersized clam into water which will be at least waist deep at low tide.'

This suggestion is mentioned here to point out that clams can rebury themselves, and today, even though regulations require reburying of undersized clams, some clammers will still toss undersized clams into deeper water, thus keeping the clams from being eaten by gulls or washed up high on the beach during stormy weather. Weymouth (1923) points out that small clams can even rebury themselves when lying exposed on moist sand by manipulating their knife-edged foot.   John Fitch reports that large clams over about 5.5 inches cannot rebury themselves even when covered by water and that apparently healthy large clams have been observed lying on their sides in deeper subtidal areas of southern California.

The heaviest mortality of sublegal clams by man is probably damage by clamming forks, and in a recent survey of clam shells at Pismo Beach, Morro Bay, and at Monterey Bay most of the shell fragments along Pismo Beach beaches were probably from this source followed by gull-dropped shells. There were only a few exposed clams on Monterey Bay beaches left abandoned by clammers or by children playing with small clams dug in the intertidal zone during low tide. Some of these smaller clams are picked up by gulls; however, this is not a major source of clam mortality.

On February 22, 1975, a swath approximately 4 miles by 165 feet was surveyed from Manresa State Beach to the south parking lot at Sunset State Beach. Gaped shells, live clams, broken gull-droppped shells, and the characteristic sea otter shattered shell fragments were tallied...46 gull-dropped shells, 10 gaped shells, five live clams, and 65 "otter shells" were tallied. The "otter shells" are typically shaped fragments formed by the shell being pounded on its "edge" on another Pismo clam lying flat on the otter's chest. The two shell halves fracture, leaving the umbo and hinge ligament structures intact.

Sea otter broken shells were common in areas being foraged, but those retrieved in the intertidal zone do not reflect the quantity of clams being consumed. Most of the foraging is done subtidally. In the surveys at Pismo Beach and Oceano which are outside the sea otter's foraging range, one shell was found with this appearance within an area over a mile in length and about 100 yards in width. Possibly by some freak chance a gull-dropped shell may fracture in this manner. These characteristic shells were common at Atascadero State Beach, where sea otters had been foraging.

Fresh gull-dropped shells are readily identifiable. Usually all or nearly all the shell fragments are present at the impact area and the inner shell surface is encrusted with sand clinging to the bits of meat and mantle that may be left as well as to the sticky, unwashed inner shell surface. Most often one half of a gull-dropped shell is intact with the other half shattered into from two to six pieces. The largest gull-dropped shell measured 4.3 inch in total length; the average size was 3.0 inch.

Estimate of Pismo Clams Taken by Clammers

A rough estimate of 15,000 clammer days was calculated for Monterey Bay in April 1974 to March 1975 period. The total 1,935 clammers interviewed over the past year took 4,427 legal sized clams for an average of 2.29 clams per clamming day. This average is slightly biased to lower catch values, inasmuch as many of these clammer days were expended in areas foraged by sea otters and there was a disproportionately greater sampling effort at several of these sea otter foraged beaches. Outside the sea otter's foraging range the average catch-per-day by clammers was 3.16 clams. Using an average of 3.0 clams per day for the maximum 15,000 clammer days, about 45,000 legal clams were taken between April and March 1975 from Monterey Bay.

Illegal sized clams were reported by many observers to be of considerable magnitude this year because of the many clams present just under legal size in the subtidal area. Marine wardens encountered overlimits and take of sublegal clams, but the magnitude of this take was not great enough to affect the stocks in any way and was certainly not as great as rumored.

Warden Bob Grossi noted that about one clammer in 25 was in possession of illegal clams in September and October, but by February when clams were becoming scarce in sea otter foraging areas about 4 of every 25 clammers could be expected to possess illegal clams. Warden Ken Boettcher estimated that about 10% of the clammers in Monterey Bay possessed illegal clams and also related the increase in illegal operations as clams became scare.

There was also a greater than usual number of novice clammers present this year subsequent to Pismo clamming articles appearing in two major nationally distributed magazines. Many of these clammers did not even know how to dig for clams, what gear to use or what the regulations were. The average number of illegal clams possessed by clammers actually cited (62) by one warden was 6.3 illegal clams.

Using the high values for illegal operations of 4 clammers out of 25 being violators and each of these possessing an average of two illegal clams apiece, approximately 2,400 illegal clammers possessed around 4,800 illegal clams within the past year.

Some clams carelessly thrown on the exposed sand may be picked up by gulls or die from other causes. The 4 miles of sandy beach covered on the February 22, 1975 shell census represented about half the clamming area of Monterey Bay, and if gulls dropped as many small clams outside this area as inside, then about 100 clams may be dropped each clam tide day by gulls. There were about 50 days of low tide periods within the open season last year, thus about 5,000 clams per year may be killed by gulls in this manner. Clam fork mortality is an unknown parameter for Monterey Bay, but from evidence at Pismo Beach, several thousand clams may be killed each year in this way in Monterey Bay.

Summarizing man caused mortality, there was a maximum of 45,000 legal clams taken, another possible 4,800 illegal clams removed, and about 5,000 clams left exposed by clammers and others that were picked up by gulls and dropped, totaling 54,800 clams killed directly or indirectly by humans, not counting clams killed by clam forks, run over by beach vehicles, or broken by non-clammers. Summing up all these possible mortalities, it may be suggested that around 60,000 clams were killed by man's activities in Monterey Bay in the April 1974 to March 1975 period. Some of these estimates are admittedly subject to question, but whatever the extent of human mortality, clammer interview data demonstrated clearly that the effects of all these activities did not adversely affect clam stocks in Monterey Bay.

Catch per hour values for both legal and sublegal sized Pismo clams were nearly the same at the end of the season as at the beginning at beaches outside the sea otter's foraging range, which were also the areas of heaviest clamming activity. The sharp decline in catches as sea otters moved into the Palm Beach and south Sunset State Beach areas are attributed solely to sea otter foraging and not to effects of clamming activity.

Foraging of Pismo Clams by Sea Otters

. . .Shell fragment data and ground and aerial census observations demonstrate that the main concentration or aggregation of sea otters remains somewhat cohesive, at least when foraging, and instead of at first spreading out over the entire food-rich beach area from the Salinas River to Capitola, they have progressively foraged from south to north reducing clam densities to very low levels before moving into another dense clam area.

This immigrating behavior somewhat parallels that displayed by sea otters as they moved progressively along rocky reef and kelp bed habitat from the center of their range. Along these Pismo clam beaches there are no kelp beds and reef areas yet the animals appear to be exhibiting some sort of transitional territorial or homing behavior that brings them back each day to where they foraged previously. Ground and aerial observations reveal that these sea otters forage primarily in the early morning and late afternoon periods with a few animals remaining in the surf area to forage throughout the day. Several observations made of the intertidal zone after a high tide early morning feeding revealed numbers of large broken shells with pieces of clam meat still attached. Two chunks of clam meat and viscera approximately 1 inch in diameter were found lying on the sand, and several gulls were beginning to pick up other scattered bits of clam meats. Gulls often remain with foraging sea otters along these beaches picking up scraps from the water near the otter, indicating not all meats are consumed from each clam by the otters.

After feeding, the otters swim offshore from ¼ to 2 miles, where pairs of animals or from five to six may remain in close proximity to each other. Several more animals may be some 100 yards away with still other individuals or pairs resting from up to ¼ to ½ mile away. This loose aggregation has been noted on each of the aerial flights conducted in midday off Monterey Bay beaches and off Atascadero State Beach. The animals off Atascadero tend to remain closer to shore, most of them remaining within ¼ mile of the breaker line.

On days when observations were made during both morning and afternoon feeding periods, sea otters returned to the same area as foraged in the morning... During a heavy freshwater runoff period in late January 1975 the Pajaro River deposited muddy water in the surf zone where otters had been foraging, and for 2 days no sea otters were seen foraging along the area from Manresa State Beach to Palm Beach... Clam shell fragment distribution suggests that when foraging at night the otters remained in the same area frequented during daytime, as no large numbers of "otter shells" were found outside the area where daytime foraging was observed.

To estimate the number of clams eaten by the sea otters requires several assumptions that cannot be adequately tested. The parameters yielding this rough estimate include number of animals foraging between April 1974 and March 1975, the approximate size of the animals, the number of clams seen eaten per feeding period, the total amount of food consumed each day, distribution of the sea otters, and food items they consumed other than clams. The sea otters along the clam beaches appear to be immature independent animals, probably mostly males. These animals are exceptionally active compared to animals foraging in rocky reef and kelp bed areas and exhibit the typical behavior of young aggressive males.

Kirkpatrick et al (1955) and Malkovitch (1937) found that young animals consume more food per day by body weight than larger animals. Twenty to 30 pound animals consumed from to 29 to 36% of their weight per day. Feeding experiments by these and other researchers indicate that an average sized animal of about 55 pounds consumes about 25% of its weight per day.

Using a conservative average weight of only 40 pounds for the sea otters foraging along Monterey clam beaches and a 30% of body weight per day consumption of food, each sea otter consumes about 12 pounds of meat per day. Mark Stephenson observed an otter of Moss Landing consuming 24 large Pismo clams in a 2 hour and 15 minute period in an incomplete feeding and 22 clams were observed consumed by a sea otter at Atascadero State Beach in a single incomplete feeding (Wild and Ames 1974).

Assuming that sea otters forage twice each day, then at least 50 clams per day would be consumed by each otter at the rates of feeding observed above. Recent observations in Carmel Bay and off Monterey by Steven Shimek disclosed a feeding period during the middle of the night. It is not known, however, how many times an individual sea otter forages each day or night. Some observations indicate several feedings, but others possibly only one. This is a little known phenomenon of the sea otter behavior and most likely the habitat being foraged and volume of items available may determine the number of times an otter feeds each day.

It is known that sea otters in captivity consume from 36% of their weight per day as young growing animals and as little as 15% per day of their body weight as old mature animals and that animals in captivity and in the wild feed several times a day.

If a young 40-pound sea otter consumes shellfish meats at the rate of 30% of its body weight each day, then at least 12 pounds of meats would be required per day. Pismo clams measuring 4.5 inches total length, the average large sized clams in the subtidal area, contain an average of 0.148 lbs of meat (2⅓ ounces). If a sea otter requires 12 pounds of meat per day, then at least 80 4.5 inch clams per day would be eaten.

Twenty-five clams of this size would supply only about 4 pounds of food, so at this rate at least three feedings per day would be required for minimum daily requirements of energy. Pismo clams are the primary food item being foraged along these beaches. Mark Stephenson noted in two separate foraging observations that 92.3 and 27.5% of food items by numbers were Pismo clams, the remainder being spiny mole crabs... About five large spiny mole crabs contain an equal wet weight of viscera, egg mass, and "body" meat as the biomass of one 4.5 inch Pismo clam...

Other evidence that Pismo clams are the preferred items sought along these beaches and that spiny mole crabs are incidental by preference is that spiny mole crabs are apparently about as numerous after the sea otter front has depleted the Pismo clam stocks and moved to new areas as before... A few sea otters continue to forage these depleted beaches and have been observed foraging on both Pismo clams and mole crabs. Assuming the "body" meats are eaten along with the viscera and egg mass a small 40 pound sea otter would have to consume at least 400 spiny mole crabs per day to meet its minimum daily energy requirements; assuming the food value of mole crabs is comparable to the value of food items used in energetics experiments. The large numbers of mole crabs present and the few numbers of sea otters remaining indicates this food source is not sufficient to maintain a resident population of sea otters.

Assuming a young sea otter could actually exist on only 10 pounds of food daily and only large 4.5 inch clams were eaten, then at least 67 clams would be required per day. If 5% of the daily food by volume is of crabs, then 9.5 pounds of clams at 0.15 pounds per clam would total at least 63 large clams needed per day per sea otter. This is the lowest possible number of clams a sea otter must consume per day as determined from all the data known about sea otter food requirements.

Summary

1. A statewide clammer census conducted in January 1975 revealed that except for one small area near Pismo Beach pier, Pismo clam stocks at the major clamming beaches in Orange and Los Angeles counties, the Pismo Beach and Morro Bay areas, and in northern Monterey Bay are in healthy condition with good catches being recorded. Pismo clam stocks appear

to be harvested on a sustainable annual yield and reproduction is above average in recent years. The highest catch-per-day values were recorded near Newport Pier, Oceano, Morro Spit, and Seacliff State Beach in Monterey Bay.

2. Inside the sea otter's foraging range virtually no clams were taken. About 4 clams per 100 clammers were recorded at the four beach areas where sea otters had foraged for more than a year. These precluded beaches are Atascadero State Beach, Salinas River State Beach, Jetty Beach at Moss Landing and Smudowski State Beach. At Palm Beach and Sunset State Beach, where sea otters were foraging during the census period, catches were down to about 22 clams per 100 clammers. Outside the sea otter's range in Monterey Bay, 302 clams per 100 clammers were recorded.

3. Trench transect and 15-minute dig data collected by Department biologists in 1953, 1966, 1968, 1970, and 1974 revealed that recruitment of young clams was good in 1953, poor in the 1966 and 1968 studies, and exceptionally good in the 1974 surveys. The dominant hatches contributing to the good recruitment measured in 1974 are the 1969, 1970, and 1971 year classes in Monterey Bay.

The healthy stocks of legal and sublegal clams from 4 to 6 inches in length are from an accumulation of clams from many year classes with the 1962 and 1963 year classes contributing to a major portion of the legal catch. Sublegal clams in the 4 to 5 inch category are also depleted by sea otter foraging, but the dominant size group of 1.5 to 3.5 inch clams in the intertidal and shallow subtidal areas are not as greatly reduced.

4. An estimated 15,000 clammer days were expended in Monterey Bay from April 1974 through March 1975. About 45,000 legal clams were taken, an additional 4,800 clams left lying exposed on the sand by clammers and picnickers were picked up by gulls and dropped to break the shell, and another 5,000 illegal clams were estimated taken by clammers, totaling around 54,800 clams killed directly or indirectly by humans in this 12 month period. Adding several thousand clams possibly killed

by clam fork damage and other human activities, around 60,000 Pismo clams may have been removed from Monterey Bay clam stocks due to man's activities during this one year study period.

5. Sea otters moved into the Potrero Road beach area in April of 1973 and foraged progressively northward removing most of the larger clams throughout the surf zone. Instead of spreading out over the entire food-rich surf zone, the sea otters moved along a "migrant front", progressively foraging clams to low levels before moving into the next dense population of clams. Pismo clams made up from 28 to 92% by numbers of food items along these beaches and considering the relatively small biomass of a mole crab Pismo clams probably contributed to over 95% of the diet by volume. Sea otters foraging along these beaches rested outside the surf zone up to 2 miles offshore, returning to the area previously foraged.

6. Numbers of sea otters ranged from 10 in June of 1973 to 46 in January 1975. Except for a two-day period after a heavy freshwater runoff of muddy water in January 1975, sea otters were observed foraging during every ground and aerial census of these beaches. A rough conservative estimate of the number of clams consumed by sea otters in the April 1974 to March 1975 period was 520,000 clams. Considering that some sea otters continue to frequent areas previously heavily foraged, it can be expected that the small sublegal clams remaining in the intertidal zone will not reach legal size in sufficient numbers to develop another recreational fishery as long as sea otters are present.[14]

SECTION SEVEN
. . .IN CLOSING

TWENTY-NINE
. . .In Closing

THE SAGA of a fellow passenger on our spaceship Earth has been traced in the preceding chapters. He shares areas of our environment. He is one whose behavior many of us appreciate because occasionally it approaches some human qualities and because his intelligence is superior. He competes for some of those natural resources of "ours" that we value for economic, recreational or gastronomic reasons.

Too, this fellow creature has polarized the opinion of one of our human communities with some claiming that the otter has inalienable rights to repopulate his historic territory, of which our human predecessors deprived his species. Others claim that a compromise is possible which can produce shellfish for sport and commercial picking while giving the otter an exclusive but limited range along the California coast. That both communities have compelling and well-defined goals and views, there is no question.

What might be the majority position of the other humans in our compartment of the spaceship is unknown, and because increasingly more regulations are shaped by public opinion, this is unfortunate. One purpose of this book is to attempt to display the controversy, catching the eye and ear of more passengers, because the otters belong to all of us passengers. Thus we are his guardians, stewards.

The cherished hope is that the result might be a broadening of the public opinion base, and with it perhaps the materialization of a solution to this monumental conundrum. The burden of the unriddling of the enigma which could lead to the best management of the sea otter seems too great for a public agency to assume (even a pair of them). A decade ago perhaps not, but today, yes. And the reason is apparent.

At least one thing appears certain about the otter's future: on his horizon is a protracted adventure epic complete with requisite highs, lows, heroes, villains, upheavals and lulls, guaranteeing that the drama is "to be continued."

As this goes to press early in June, 1979, between seventy and eighty otters have swung around Pt. San Luis and have reached Shell Beach and Pismo Beach evoking both consternation and pleasure among residents.

What the tally of these emotions is cannot be divined simply by the letters-to-the-editor. However, merchants have urged individual appeals to the Department of the Interior as well as to the district's congressional delegation. The Chamber of Commerce has invited the public to assemble for the purpose of questioning some of the CDFG biologists charged with the otter-tagging program.

The Chamber appealed to the San Luis Obispo County Board of of Supervisors, which included in a June meeting an hour for the contending forces in the resource conflict to assume advocate roles. Whether or not the Board will endeavor to help resolve the issue is unknown, but a hearing was held and another scheduled. The Pismo Beach Chamber of Commerce representative reviewed to the Board the oft-repeated example of the decimated red abalone fishery at Estero Bay, laying full blame on Enhydra. The otter's champions insisted that the otter population must be allowed broad dispersal for survival's sake, listing the incipient dangers of an oil spill and explaining that an otter contaminated by crude oil cannot be rescued.

The friends repeated that loss of a colony offers a slim chance of replacement by its Alaskan or Aleutian cousins. Besides (they continued), the Marine Mammal Commission and the CDFG have never held the anticipated meeting to choose a site on which to plant a reserve colony. Lastly, the mammal's protectors explained the obstacle in the path of returning the guardianship of the otter to the State: the long list of criteria laid down by the Commission to satisfy. (For a year Alaska has attempted to do precisely this in her effort to regain management of her former otter colonies.)

And so goes the otter drama, year, decade, century, after year, decade, century. Which turns the drama will take only Time will tell. . . Time, and more Time. . .

THE END

APPENDIX

Text of the Federal Fish and Wildlife Permit issued by the U.S. Fish and Wildlife service to the Director, California Department of Fish and Game, effective August 26, 1977 and expiring September 30, 1979.

The permit for marine mammal scientific research authorized activity in California and adjacent Pacific coastal waters. The conditions and authorizations are quoted from the permit as follows:

A. General conditions set out in subpart D of 50 CFR 13, and specific conditions contained in federal regulations cited in block #2 above, are hereby made a part of this permit. All activities authorized herein must be carried out in accord with and for the purposes described in the application submitted. Continued validity, or renewal of this permit is subject to complete and timely compliance with all applicable conditions, including the filing of all required information and reports.

B. The validity of this permit is also conditioned upon strict observance of all applicable foreign, state, local or other federal law.

C. Valid for use by permittee named above and any person designated in writing by the permittee.

D. Authorized to conduct the following activities with sea otters (*Enhydra lutris*), as specified in Block 10, for scientific research:

1. capture, tag, weigh, sex, measure, take blood samples from, and release, as described in the application, 100 sea otters (approximately 50 males and 50 females) from throughout the range each year for two years. Initial tagging efforts should be confined to the northern portion of the range so that the effects of capture, handling, and tagging activities on the behavior of the animals can be distinguished from the effects of translocation activities. Applicant must attempt to tag mostly young animals. Wooly pups, older animals, and females with with wooly pups will not be intentionally captured. It is recommended that all animals that are captured, except pups, be tagged. For purposes of this permit, animals less than 15 pounds should be considered pups. All animals should be double tagged and colors should be used in such a manner that individuals can be identified with respect to their sex and the area where they were tagged. The applicant may use the plastic ear tag in the course of these efforts, as described in the application, but the effects of this tag on the animals must be monitored closely;

2. capture, tag on the hind flipper, sex, weigh, measure, take blood samples from, transport, hold, and release as described in the application, up to a total of 40 animals (approximately 30 males and 10 females), including the following specific activities to be undertaken successively: a) capture six non-reproductive animals at the southern migrant front of the population, transport, hold, and release the animals, at a site north of the northern migrant front of the population, as described in the application. The release site should be significantly northward of the location of the main northern migrant front and should be determined in consultation with the Fish and Wildlife Service and the Marine Mammal Commission. It is suggested that the Sand Hill Bluff area is an appropriate release site for consideration;
(b) capture 4 independent animals (2 males and 2 females without pups) in the Monterey-Carmel area, and transport, hold and release the animals as describe in the application, at the site described in (a) above;
(c) capture 4 independent animals (2 males and 2 females without pups) in the area from Yankee Point to Point Sur, and transport, hold, and release the animals as described in the application, at the site described in (a) above;

(d) capture 12 animals (6 males and 6 females without pups) in the area from Esalen to Cape San Martin, and transport, hold, and release the animals as described in the application, at the site described in (a) above; and

(e) after evaluation of the results of the activities described above, capture 14 animals, including up to 6 animals from the southern migrant front and transport, hold and release the animals as described in the application, at the site described in (a) above.

3. Authorization to translocate sea otters is limited to 40 animals during the first year following the issuance date of this permit. Additional animals may be authorized after consultation with the Director, Fish and Wildlife Service and the Marine Mammal Commission.

E. The Regional Director, U.S. Fish and Wildlife Service office (503-429-4050) must be notified seven days before commencing the permitted activities.

F. Acceptance of this permit authorizes inspection per 50 CFR 13.47.

G. Permittee must have a copy of this permit in his possession while conducting the activities authorized.

H. The loss, death, or destruction of the sea otters shall be reported within 24 hours to the Regional Director, U.S. Fish and Wildlife Service, Portland (503-429-4050) and in writing to the Dept. of the Interior (FWS), Federal Wildlife Permit Office, Washington, D.C. 20240, within 10 days.

I. A duplicate of this permit must be attached to the container in which the sea otters are placed for storage, supervision, or care.

J. Permittee shall maintain records as required in 50 CFR 13.46.

K The Portland FWS office will provide instructions for the disposition of any specimens salvaged.

L. The sea otters and/or any progeny may not be sold, donated, or transferred unless the receiver has first been issued authorization by the Director.

M. Activities conducted under authority of this permit must be for official business only.

REFERENCES FOR *SEA OTTER*

1   Marine Resources Technical Report #20 (Wild and Williams), *A Report On The Sea Otter, Enhydra lutris lutris, In California,* 1974
2   *Otter Raft* #15, Spring, 1976. Published by Friends of the Sea Otter, P.O. Box FF, Carmel, California, 93921
3   Snow, H.J., *In Forbidden Seas,* 1910, (Edward Arnold, London)
4   Kenyon, Karl W., *The Sea Otter In The Eastern Pacific Ocean,* 1969 (U.S. Bureau of Sport Fisheries and Wildlife, North American Fauna Series, No. 68)
5   McCracken, Harold, *Hunters Of The Stormy Sea,* 1957 (Doubleday, Garden City, New York)
6   von Langsdorff, Georg H., *Voyages And Travels In Various Parts Of The World,* 1814 (H. Colburn, London; Gregg Press, Ridgewood, N.J., 1968)
7   Warner, Colonel, J. J., *Reminiscences Of Early California From 1831 To 1846,* Southern California Historical Society Annual Publications 1907-1908.
8   Antrim, James E., Cornell, Lanny, monograph: *The Rehabilitation of Sea Otters,* 1977 (Sea World, San Diego, California, 92109)
9   *Otter Raft* #20 (Winter 1978) Published by Friends of the Sea Otter, P.O. Box FF, Carmel, California 93921
10 Davis, Dr. Betty S., *The Southern Sea Otter* (Pacific Discovery Magazine, April/May, 1977, California Academy of Sciences, San Francisco)
11 *Otter Raft* #3 (June, 1970) Published by Friends of the Sea Otter, P.O. Box FF, Carmel, California 93921
12 *Otter Raft* #4 (December, 1970) Published by Friends of the Sea Otter, P.O. Box FF, Carmel, California 93921
13 *Otter Raft* #6 (December, 1971) Published by Friends of the Sea Otter, P.O. Box FF, Carmel, California 93921
14 Marine Resources Technical Report #31 (Miller, Hardwick, Dahlstrom), *Pismo Clams And Sea Otters,* 1975

BIBLIOGRAPHY

Atherton, Gertrude F. 1969. *Rezanov.* Reprint of 1906 ed. Boston, Mass: The Gregg Press, Inc.

Bailey, Jane H. 1973. *The Sea Otter's Struggle.* Follett Publishing Company, Chicago. Reprint 1978 El Moro Publications, P.O. Box 965, Morro Bay, CA 93442

Barabash-Nikiforov, I.I. 1947. *The Sea Otter (Kalan).* Soviet Ministrov RSFSR. Translated from Russian by Dr. A. Birron and Z.S. Cole. Israel Program for Scientific Translations.

Coues, Elliot. 1970 *Fur-Bearing Animals of North America.* Reprint of 1877 ed. New York: Arno Publishing Company.

Cox, Keith W. 1962. *California Abalone, Family Haliotidae.* California Fish and Game, Fish Bulletin 118. CDFG, Sacramento, California.

Daugherty, Anita E. 1966. *Marine Mammals of California.* California Department of Fish and Game, Sacramento, California.

Davis, Betty S. *The Southern Sea Otter* 1977. Pacific Discovery Magazine, April/May. California Academy of Science, San Francisco, California.

Ebert, Earl E. 1968 *A Food Habits Study Of The Southern Sea Otter, Enhydra lutris nereis.* "California Fish and Game", vol. 54, no. 1.

Eldredge, Zoeth S. (ed.) 1915. *History Of California.* Century History Company, New York.

Fisher, Edna N. 1939. *Habits Of The Southern Sea Otter.* Journal of Mammalogy,, vol. 20, no. 1.

_____1940. *Early Life Of A Sea Otter Pup.* Journal of Mammalogy, vol. 21, no. 2.

Hafen, Leroy. 1965. *Mountain Men Of The Fur Trade Of The Far West.* A. H. Clark Company, Glendale.

Kenyon, Karl W. 1969. *The Sea Otter In The Eastern Pacific Ocean.* North American Fauna (series), Number 68, U.S. Bureau of Sport Fisheries and Wildlife. 1975 Dover Press, New York.

McCracken, Harold 1957. *Hunters Of The Stormy Sea.* Doubleday, Garden City, N.J.

Miller, D., Hardwick J., and Dahlstrom, W. 1975. *Pismo Clams And Sea Otters.* Marine Resources Technical Report #31, California Department of Fish and Game, Sacramento, California.

Miller, P. and L.G. 1967. *Lost Heritage Of Alaska.* World Publishing Company, Cleveland, Ohio.

Ogden, Adele 1941. *The California Sea Otter Trade 1784-1848.* University of California Press, Berkeley and Los Angeles.

"Otter Raft" 1969- Quarterly published by The Friends of the Sea Otter, P.O. Box FF, Carmel, California, 93921.

Paca, Lillian G. 1965. *California Sea Otter.* D'Angelo Publishing Co., Carmel, CA.

Ricketts, E.F. and Calvin J. 1968. *Between Pacific Tides,* Fourth Edition. Joel W. Hedgepeth, ed. Stanford, California: Stanford University Press.

von Langsdorff, Georg H. 196. *Voyages And Travels In Various Parts Of The World.* Gregg Press, Boston, Mass.

Wild, P. and Ames J. 1974. *A Report On The Sea Otter Enhydra lutris lutris., In California.* Marine Resources Technical Report #20. California Department of Fish and Game, Sacramento, California.

NOTES